The darkness fell and out in the road beyond the great gate a lonely little boy stood looking down the road at the last of the departing guests. He stood with hands clasped, thinking of a life of misery which had been predicted, thinking of the horrors of war which he did not understand, thinking of the insensate persecution yet to come. He stood there, alone in all the world . . . He stood there and the night grew darker, and no one came to seek him and lead him back. At last he lay down by the side of the road and in minutes there was a purring beside his head and a great big cat lay down beside him. The boy put his arms around the animal and drifted off to sleep, but the cat was alert, watching, guarding. . . .

Also by T. Lobsang Rampa

As It Was!

T. Lobsang Rampa

CORGI BOOKS
A DIVISION OF TRANSWORLD PUBLISHERS LTD

AS IT WAS!

A CORGI BOOK 0 552 10087 0

First publication in Great Britain

PRINTING HISTORY
Corgi edition published 1976

Corgi Books are published by
Transworld Publishers Ltd.,
Century House, 61-63 Uxbridge Road,
Ealing, London, W.5.
Made and printed in the United States of America
by Arcata Graphics,
Buffalo, New York

Dedicated to The City of Calgary, where I have had peace and quiet and freedom from interference in my personal affairs. Thank you, City of Calgary.

AS IT WAS!

. . . . . .

. . .

.

FOREWORD ...

All "the best" books have a Foreword, so it is very necessary that THIS book have one. After all, Authors are quite entitled to regard their own books as The Best. Let me start The Best with an explanation of WHY I chose my title.

"As It Was!" Now why would he use such a silly title? He says in other books that he ALWAYS writes the truth! Sure, sure, you shall have your explanation, so just Keep Calm (should be in six-inch capitals) and READ ON.

All my books ARE true, and I have maintained that fact in face of relentless persecution and calumny. But throughout the ages sane, sensible people have been persecuted and even tortured and killed for telling it As It was! A Very Wise Man was almost burnt at the stake for daring to assert that the Earth revolved around the Sun instead of—as the Priests taught—that the Earth was the centre of Creation and all planets revolved around it. The poor fellow had a terrible time, being stretched on the Rack and all that, and saved being cooked only by recanting.

Then there have been people who inadvertently levitated at the wrong moment in front of the wrong people with the wrong results; they have been bumped off in various spectacular ways for letting it be known that they were different from the common horde. Some of "the horde" ARE common, too, especially if they are pressmen!

Humans of the worst type—you know who THEY are! —just LOVE to drag everyone down to the same level; they just cannot bear to think that anyone is different from they, so, like maniacs, they cry "destroy! destroy!" And instead of trying to prove a person right—they must always try to prove him wrong. The Press in particular like to start witch-hunting and persecute a person so that sensation may be stirred up. The morons of the Press lack the wits to think that there MIGHT be "something in it after all!"

Edward Davis, "America's Toughest Cop," wrote in True Magazine dated January 1975: "The Media in general is really composed of a bunch of frustrated fiction writers. Putting it another way, Journalism is filled with Picasso types who get out their paint boxes and construct a picture that's supposed to be me, but which nobody recognises except the guy with the tar brush and feathers." Mr. Davis, it is very clear, does not like the Press. Nor do I. Both of us have good reason not to. A pressman said to me: "Truth? Truth never sold a paper. Sensation does. We do not bother with truth; we sell sensation."

Ever since the publication of "The Third Eye"—a TRUE book!—"strange creatures have crawled out of the woodwork" and with pens dipped in venom have written books and articles attacking me. Self-styled "experts" declared THIS to be false, while others of the genre declared THIS to be true but THAT false. No two "experts" could agree.

Itinerant "investigators" toured around interviewing people who had never met me, fabricating wholly imaginary stories. The "investigators" never met me either. Pressmen, desperate for sensation, concocted "interviews" which never took place. Mrs. Rampa, in an entirely fabricated "interview" was quoted—misquoted—as saying the book was fiction. She did not say it. She has never said it. We both say—All my books are TRUE.

But neither press, radio, or publishers, have EVER permitted me the opportunity of giving my side of the matter. Never! Nor have I been asked to appear on T.V. or radio and tell the Truth! Like many before me I have been persecuted for being "different" from the majority. So Humanity destroys those who could help Mankind with special knowledge, or special experiences. We, the Unusual, could, if allowed, push back the Frontiers of Knowledge and advance man's understanding of Man.

The press report me as small and hairy, big and bald,

10

tall and short, thin and fat. Also—according to "reliable" press reports, I am English, Russian, a German sent to Tibet by Hitler, Indian, etc. "RELIABLE" press reports! ANYTHING—anything at all except the Truth—but that is contained within my books.

So many lies have been told about me. So much distorted imagination has been exercised, so much suffering has been caused, so much misery—But here in this book is Truth. I am telling it

As It Was!

Book One

As it was in the beginning.

CHAPTER ONE

The old old man leaned back wearily against a supporting pillar. His back was numb with the pain of sitting long hours in one cramped position. His eyes were blurred with the rheum of age. Slowly he rubbed his eyes with the back of his hands and peered around. Papers—papers, nothing but papers littered the table before him. Papers covered with strange symbols and masses of crabbed figures. Dimly seen people moved before him awaiting his orders.

Slowly the old man climbed to his feet, fretfully thrusting aside helping hands. Shaking with the weight of years he moved to a nearby window. Shivering a little by the opening, he tucked his ancient robe tighter around his sparse frame. Bracing his elbows against the stonework he stared around. Cursed with the ability to see afar when his work demanded that he see near, he now could see to the farthest limits of the Plain of Lhasa.

The day was warm for Lhasa. The willow trees were at their best, with leaves showing the youngest green. Small catkins, or pussy-willow, lent a pleasant myriad of yellow streaks to the green and brown background. Four hundred feet below the old man the colours blended most harmoniously with the gleam of the pellucid water showing through the lower branches.

The old Chief Astrologer mused on the land before him, contemplated the mighty Potala in which he lived and which he so rarely left, and then only for the most pressing matters. No, no, he thought, let me not think of THAT yet; let me rest my eyes by enjoying the view.

There was much activity in the Village of Shö which clustered so snugly at the foot of the Potala. Brigands had been caught while robbing traders in the high mountain passes and had been brought to the Hall of Justice in the

Village. Justice had already been dispensed to other offenders; men convicted of some serious crime or other walked away from the Hall, their chains clanking in tune with their steps. Now they would have to wander from place to place begging for their food, for, chained, they could not easily work.

The old Astrologer gazed wistfully toward the Great Cathedral of Lhasa. Long had he contemplated a visit to renew boyhood memories; his official duties had for too many years prevented any diversions for pleasure alone. Sighing, he started to turn away from the window, then he stopped and looked hard into the distance. Beckoning to an attendant, he said, "Coming along the Dodpal Linga, just by the Kesar, I seem to recognise that boy, isn't it the Rampa boy?" The attendant nodded, "Yes, Reverend Sir, that is the Rampa boy and the manservant Tzu. The boy whose future you are preparing in that horoscope." The old Astrologer smiled wryly as he looked down on the figure of the very small boy and the immense almost seven-foot tall manservant from the Province of Kham. He watched as the two ill-matched figures, one on a small pony and the other on a large horse, rode up until an outcrop of rock from the Mountain hid them from view. Nodding to himself, he turned back to the littered table.

"So THIS," he murmured, "will be square with THAT. Hmmn, so for more than sixty years he will have much suffering because of the adverse influence of—" His voice lapsed into a low drone as he rifled through countless papers, making notes here, and scratching-out there. This old man was the most famous astrologer of Tibet, a man well versed in the mysteries of that venerable art. The astrology of Tibet is far different from that of the West. Here in Lhasa the date of conception was correlated with the date of birth. A progressed horoscope also would be done for the date on which the complete "work" was to be delivered. The Chief Astrologer would predict the Life Path of the famous, and of significant members of those families. The government itself would be advised by astrologers, as would the Dalai Lama. But THIS was not the astrology of the West, which seems to be prostituted to the sensational press.

At long, low tables, priest-astrologers sat cross-legged checking figures and their relationship to each other. Charts were drawn of the heavenly configurations extant at the time of conception, time of birth, time of delivery of the horoscope reading, which was known well in advance, and for every year of "the life of the subject" a full chart and annual delineation was prepared. Then there was the blending of the whole into one very large report.

Tibetan paper is all handmade and forms quite thick sheets roughly eight inches from top to bottom by about two feet to two feet six broad. Western paper for writing is longer from top to bottom than it is broad; Tibetan paper is the opposite. The pages of books are not bound but are held in a pile between two sheets of wood. In the West such books would soon be ruined, with pages lost or torn. In Tibet paper is sacred and is treated with extreme care; to waste paper is a serious offence and to tear a page was to waste paper—hence the extreme care. A lama would be reading, but he would have a small acolyte to stand by him. The wooden top sheet of the book would be removed with great care and would be placed face down on the left of the Reader. Then, after reading the top sheet, the page would reverently be removed by the acolyte and placed face down on the top cover. After the reading was finished, the sheets would be carefully levelled, and the book would be tied together with tapes.

So was the horoscope prepared. Sheet after sheet was written on or drawn upon. The sheet was put aside to dry—for it was an offence to waste paper by smudging. Then, at last, after perhaps six months, for time did not matter, the horoscope was ready.

Slowly the acolyte, in this case a young monk with already several years of experience, reverently lifted the sheet and placed it face down upon its companion on the leaf. The old Astrologer lifted the new sheet thus exposed. "Tch, tch," he grumbled, "this ink is going a bad colour before it is even exposed to the light. We must have this

17

page rewritten." With that he picked up one of his "scribble sticks" and made a hasty notation.

These scribble sticks were an invention dating back many thousands of years, but they were made in precisely the same manner as they had been made two or three thousand years before. There was, in fact, a legend to the effect that Tibet had once been by the side of a shining sea and support was lent to the legend by the frequent finding of sea-shells, fossilised fish, and many other items which could have come only from a warmer country then beside the sea. There were buried artefacts of a long-dead race, tools, carvings, jewellery. All these, together with gold, could be found in great profusion by the side of the rivers that ran through the country.

But now the scribble sticks were made in exactly the same way as they had been made previously. A large mass of clay was obtained and then monks sallied forth and picked from willow trees suitable saplings, thin pieces of twig about half as thick as one's little finger and perhaps a foot long. These were very carefully gathered and then were taken back to a special department of the Potala. Here all the twigs would be carefully examined and graded, the straight flawless ones would have particular care devoted to them, they would be peeled and then wrapped in clay, much caution being exercised to ensure that the twigs were not bent.

Those twigs which had a slight bend or twist were also wrapped in clay because they would be suitable for junior monks and acolytes to use in their own writings. The bundles of clay, each with a seal-impression showing which was super class (for the highest lamas and the Inmost One himself), and then first class for high class lamas, and second class for ordinary use, would have a very small hole made through the clay so that steam generated during a heating process could escape and thus obviate the bursting of the clay wrapping.

Now the clay would be laid on racks in a large chamber. For a month or so they would just lie there with the moisture evaporating in the low-humidity atmosphere.

Sometime between four to six months later the clay bundles would be removed and transferred to a fire—the fire would also be used for cooking purposes, heating water, and things like that—and carefully placed so that they were right in the reddest part of the fire. For a day the temperature would be maintained and then that fire would be permitted to die out. When it was cold the clay bundles would be broken open, the waste clay thrown away, and the carbonised willow sticks (charcoal) would now be ready for the highest use which is the dissemination of true knowledge.

The willow sticks which had been determined as unsuitable for conversion into charcoal sticks would have been used to help the fires drying out the clay of the better sticks. The fires were of well-dried yak dung and any odd wood which happened to be around. But again, wood was never used for burning if it could be of use for some other "more noble" purpose because wood was in very short supply in Tibet.

Scribble sticks, then, were that commodity which in the Western world are known as charcoal sticks and which are used by artists in their black and white drawings. But ink also was required in Tibet, and for that another sort of wood was used, again wrapped in clay. This was heated much longer and subjected to a much higher temperature. Then, after several days when the fires were extinguished and the clay balls raked from the now cold firebed and broken open, a very black residue would be found inside; almost pure carbon.

The carbon would be taken and very, very carefully examined for anything which was not black carbon. Then it would be put in a piece of fairly coarse mesh cloth which would be tightened and tightened over a piece of stone which had a depression in it, which had, in effect, a trough in it. The trough would be possibly eighteen inches by twelve inches and perhaps two inches deep. Monks of the domestic class would pummel the cloth in the bottom of the trough so that gradually a very fine carbon dust was formed. Eventually that would be mixed with a hot gum

19

from certain trees which grew in the area, it would be stirred and stirred and stirred until the result was a black gooey mass. Then it would be allowed to dry in cakes, afterwards when one wanted ink one just rubbed one of these cakes in a special stone container and a little water would be added to it. The result would be an ink which was of a rusty-brown colour.

Official documents and the highly important astrological charts were never prepared from ink of this common base, instead there was a piece of very highly polished marble which was suspended at an angle of about forty-five degrees, and below it there would be perhaps a dozen butter-lamps sputtering away, the wicks would be made too long—too high—so that the lamps gave off a thick black smoke. The smoke would hit the polished marble and would immediately condense into a black mass. Eventually when a suitable thickness had built up a young monk would tip the plate of marble and scoop off all the accumulation of "lamp black" before restoring the plate to its forty-five degree angle so that more carbon could be collected.

From trees a resinous gum would be collected and would be put in a container which would be very thoroughly heated so that the gum acquired the consistency of water and became much clarified. From the top of the gum, merrily boiling and seething away, a thick residue of scum would be scraped leaving an absolutely clear, slightly yellow, liquid. Into that would be stirred a whole mass of "lamp black" until the result was a fairly stiff paste. Then the stuff would be ladled out and spread on stone to cool and solidify. For the highest lamas and officials the lumps would be cut into rectangles and made into a fairly presentable mass, but the lower echelon of monks were glad to get any shape of ink slab. This was used as was the first type, that is, a special piece of stone with a recess, or small trough, was used, and into it was scraped some of the small block of ink. Then it was mixed with water until a suitable consistency was obtained.

There were, of course, no steel pens in Tibet, no fountain pens, no ball pens, instead willow twigs were used which had been carefully skinned and made smooth and the ends slightly fluffed so that, in effect, they were like brushes with very, very short bristles. The sticks were then carefully dried—very carefully indeed to avoid cracking or warping—and then when they were dry enough to prevent splitting they were put on hot stone which had the effect of fire-hardening them so that they could be handled with impunity and so that they would last quite a long time. Tibetan writing, then, is more Tibetan brushing because the characters, the ideographs, are written with a brush-form in somewhat the same way as Chinese or Japanese people write.

But the old Astrologer was muttering away about the poor quality of ink on a page. He continued reading, and then found that he was reading about the death of the subject of the horoscope. Tibetan astrology covers all aspects, life—living—death. Carefully he went through his predictions, checking and re-checking, because this was a prediction for the member of a very important family, a prediction for a person who was important not merely because of his family connections but important in his own right because of the task allotted to him.

The old man sat back, his bones creaking with weariness. With a shudder of apprehension he recalled that his own death was precariously near. This was his last great task, the preparation of a horoscope in such detail as he had never done before.

The conclusion of this task and the successful declaiming of his reading would result in the loosening of the bonds of the flesh, and the early termination of his own life. He wasn't afraid of death; death was merely a period of transition as he knew; but transition or no transition it was still a period of change, change which the old man loathed and feared. He would have to leave his beloved Potala, he would have to vacate his coveted position of Chief Astrologer of Tibet, he would have to leave all the things that he knew, all the things which were dear to him, he would have to leave and, like a new boy at a lamasery, he would have to start again. When? He knew that! Where? He knew that too! But it was hard leaving old friends, it was hard making a change in life, because there is no death, that which we call death is merely transition from life to life.

He thought of the processes. He saw himself as he had seen others so often—dead, the immobile body no longer able to move, no longer a sentient creature, but just a mass of dead flesh supported by a mass of dead bones.

In his imagination he saw himself thus, being stripped of his robes and bundled up with his head touching his knees and his legs bent behind. In his mind's eye he saw himself being bundled on the back of a pony, wrapped in cloth, and taken away beyond the outskirts of the City of Lhasa where he would be given into the care of the Disposers of the Dead.

They would take his body and they would place it on a big flat rock, specially prepared for that purpose. He would be split open and all his organs would be taken out. The Chief of the Disposers would call aloud into the air and down would come swooping a whole flock of vultures, well accustomed to such things.

The Chief Disposer would take the heart and throw it toward the chief vulture who would gulp it down without much ado, then the kidneys, the lungs, and other organs would be cut up and thrown to the other vultures.

With blood-stained hands the Disposers would rip off the flesh from the white bones, would cut the flesh into strips and throw them too to the vultures who were clustered around like a solemn congregation of old men at a party.

With all the flesh stripped off and all the organs disposed of, the bones would be broken into small lengths and then would be pushed into holes in the rock. Then rods of rock would pound the bones until they became just a powder. The powder would be mixed with the blood from the body and with other body secretions and left on the rocks for the birds to eat. Soon, in a matter of a few hours, there would be no trace of that which had once been a man. No trace of the vultures either; they would have gone away—somewhere—until called for their grisly service on the next occasion.

The old man thought of all this, thought of the things he had seen in India where poor people were disposed of by throwing the weighted bodies into the rivers or by burying them in the earth, but the richer people who could afford wood would have their bodies burned until only the flaky ash remained and then this would be thrown into some sacred river so that the ash, and perhaps the spirit of the person, would be called back to the bosom of "Mother Earth."

He shook himself roughly and muttered, "This is no time to think of my transition, let me finish my task while I prepare the notes on the transition of this small boy." But it was not to be, there came an interruption. The old Astrologer was murmuring instructions for the whole page to be rewritten in better ink when there came the sound of hasty footfalls, and the slamming of a door. The old man looked up fretfully, he wasn't used to having interruptions of this kind, he wasn't used to having noise in the Astrological Department. This was an area of calm, of quietude, of contemplation where the loudest sound was the scraping of a fire-hardened twig across the rough surface of hand-made paper. There came the sound of raised voices. "I MUST see him, I MUST see him this instant, the Inmost One demands." Then there came the slap slap of feet upon the ground, and the rustle of stiff cloth. A lama of the Dalai Lama's household appeared clutching in his right hand a stick in a cleft of which, at the distal end, a piece of paper was seen to bear the writing of the Inmost One himself. The lama came forward, made a customary half bow to the old Astrologer, and inclined the stick in his direction so that he could remove the written missive. He did so, and frowned in dismay.

"But, but—" he muttered, "how can I go now? I am in the midst of these calculations, I am in the midst of these computations. If I have to stop at this instant—" But then he realised that there was nothing for it but to go "on

23

the instant." With a sigh of resignation he changed his old work robe for a tidier one, picked up some charts and a few scribble sticks, and turned to a monk beside him saying, "Here, boy, carry these and accompany me." Turning he walked slowly out of the room in the wake of the golden robed lama.

The golden robed lama moderated his step so that the aged one following him should not be unduly distressed. For long they traversed endless corridors, monks and lamas scurrying about their business stood respectfully aside with heads bowed as the Chief Astrologer went by them.

After a considerable walk, and mounting from floor to floor, the golden robed lama and the Chief Astrologer reached the topmost floor wherein were the apartments of the Dalai Lama himself, the Thirteenth Dalai Lama, the Inmost one, the one who was to do more for Tibet than any other Dalai Lama.

The two men turned a corner and encountered three young monks behaving in an apparently riotous manner; they were skating about with their feet wrapped in cloth. Respectfully they ceased their gambols and stood aside as the two men passed. These young men had a full-time job; there were many floors to be kept spotlessly polished, and the three young monks spent the whole of their working hours with heavy cloths around their feet, they walked and ran and slid across the vast areas of flooring, and as a result of their efforts the floor had a wondrous gleam together with the patina of antiquity. But—the floor was slippery. Considerately the golden robed lama stepped back and took the arm of the old Astrologer, knowing full well that a broken leg or a broken arm at his age would be virtual sentence of death.

Soon they came to a large sunny room in which the Great Thirteenth himself was sitting in the lotus position gazing out through a window at the panorama of Himalayan mountain ranges stretching before him and, in fact, all around the Valley of Lhasa.

The old Astrologer made his prostrations to the God-

King of Tibet. The Dalai Lama motioned for the attendants to leave, and soon he and the Chief Astrologer were alone sitting face to face on the seat-cushions used in Tibet in place of chairs.

These were old acquaintants, well versed to the ways each of the other. The Chief Astrologer knew all the affairs of State, knew all the predictions about Tibet for he, indeed, had made most of them. Now the Great Thirteenth was looking most serious because these were momentous days, days of stress, days of worry. The East India Company, a British Company, was trying to get gold and other items out of the country, and various agents and leaders of British military might were toying with the idea of invading Tibet and taking over that country but the threat of Russia in the near background prevented that drastic step being taken. It will suffice to say, though, that the British caused much turmoil and much trouble for Tibet at that stage, just as in much later years the Chinese Communists would do. So far as the Tibetans were concerned there was little to choose between the Chinese and the British, the Tibetans merely wanted to be left alone.

Unfortunately there was another more serious problem in that in Tibet at that time there were two sets of priests, one was known as the Yellow Caps and the other was known as the Red Caps. Sometimes there were violent disputes between them, and the two leaders, the Dalai Lama who was the head of the Yellow Caps, and the Panchen Lama who was the head of the Red Caps, had no love whatever for each other.

Really there was little sympathy between the two sects. The Dalai Lama's supporters at the time had the upper hand, but it had not always been so, at other times the Panchen Lama—who was soon to be forced to leave Tibet —had been in the forefront and then the country had been plunged into chaos until the Dalai Lama had been able to reinforce his claims with the aid of the Tartars and because on religious grounds the Yellow Caps had what one might term "superior sanctity."

The Inmost One—the Dalai Lama who was given that

title, and was well known as The Great Thirteenth—made many questions concerning the probable future of Tibet. The old Astrologer fumbled around in the portfolio he had with him and produced papers and charts, and together the two men pored over them.

"In less than sixty years," said the Astrologer, "Tibet as a free entity will be no more. The hereditary enemy, the Chinese, with a new form of political government will invade the country and will virtually do away with the Order of Priests in Tibet."

At the passing of the Great Thirteenth, the Dalai Lama was told, another would be chosen as a palliative to Chinese aggression. A child would be picked as being the Reincarnation of the Great Thirteenth, and irrespective of the accuracy of the choice it would first and foremost be a political choice because what would be known as the Fourteenth Dalai Lama would come from Chinese held territory.

The Inmost One was most gloomy about the whole affair, and tried to work out plans of how to save his beloved country, but, as the Chief Astrologer so accurately pointed out, much could be done to circumvent the bad horoscope of an individual but there was no known way of substantially altering the horoscope and the destiny of a whole country. A country was composed of too many different units, too many individuals who could not be moulded, nor commanded, nor persuaded to think along the same lines at the same time for the same purpose. So the fate of Tibet was known. The fate of the Wise Sayings, the Holy Books and the Holy Knowledge was not yet known, but it was thought that by suitable means a young man could be trained, given special knowledge, given special abilities, and then sent forth into the world beyond the confines of Tibet so that he could write of his knowledge and of the knowledge of Tibet. The two men continued talking, and then at last the Dalai Lama said, "And this boy, the Rampa boy, have you yet prepared the horoscope for him? I shall want you to read it at a special party at the Rampa household in two weeks from this

26

day." The Chief Astrologer shuddered. Two weeks? He would not have been ready in two months or two years if he had not been given a firm date. So, in a quavering voice, he replied, "Yes, Your Holiness, all will be ready by two weeks from this day. But this boy is going to have most unfortunate conditions during his life, suffering and torture, disowning by his own countrymen, illness—every obstacle that one can imagine is being placed in his way by evil forces and by one particular force which I, as yet, do not completely understand but which appears to be connected in some ways with the newspaper workers."

The Dalai Lama sighed noisily, and said, "Well, let us put that aside for the time being because what is inevitable cannot be altered. You will have to go through your charts again during the next two weeks to make absolutely sure of that which you are going to declaim. For the moment— let us have a game of chess, I am tired of the affairs of State."

A silver bell was tinkled, and a golden robed lama came into the room and received the order to bring the chess set and the chess board so that the two men could play. Chess was very popular with the higher intellects of Lhasa, but it is a different sort of chess from that which is played in the West. In the West when a game is started the first pawn of each party moves two steps instead of the normal one as in Tibet, and in Tibet there is no such thing as castling in which when a pawn reached the back line it could become a castle, nor was the stalemate status used, instead it was considered that a state of balance or stasis had been reached when the king was left alone without a pawn or without any other piece on the board.

The two men sat and played with endless patience, each in the warm glow of love and respect which had grown between these two, and above them on the flat roof just above the Dalai Lama's quarters the prayer flags flapped in the high mountain breeze. Further down the corridor the prayer wheels clattered, churning out their endless imaginary prayers. On the flat roofs gleams blindingly golden shot from the tombs of the previous Incarnations

27

of the Dalai Lama, for in Tibetan belief each Dalai Lama as he died merely went into transition and then returned to Earth in the body of some small boy. In Tibet transmigration was such an accepted fact of religion that it was not even worthy of comment. So up on the flat roof twelve bodies lay in twelve golden tombs, each tomb having an intricately designed roof with many spirals, whorls, and convolutions designed to delude and throw off "evil spirits."

From the golden tombs one could see across to the gleaming building of the College of Medical Science, Chakpori on Iron Mountain, the home of medicine for Tibet. Beyond there was the City of Lhasa, now on this day shining bright under the high noon sun. The sky was a deep purple, and the mountains ringing the Valley of Lhasa had spumes of pure white snow blowing from their peaks.

As the hours rolled on, marked by the growing shadows from the Western mountain range, the two men in the State apartments below sighed and reluctantly pushed aside their chess pieces for now was the time of worship, the time when the Dalai Lama had to attend to his devotions, the time when the Chief Astrologer had to return to his computations if he were to meet the dead line imposed by the Dalai Lama of two weeks.

Again the silver bell was tinkled, again a golden robed lama appeared, and with a few muttered words was directed to assist the Chief Astrologer to return to his own quarters three floors below.

The Chief Astrologer rose creakily to his aged feet, made his ritual prostrations, and left the presence of his Spiritual Chief.

CHAPTER TWO

"Oo-ee! Oo-ee! Ay-yah! Ay-yah!" said the voice in the dusk of that pleasant day. "Did you hear about that Lady Rampa? She's at it again!" There was the shuffling of feet on the road, the sound of little pebbles being rolled underfoot, and then a sigh. "Lady Rampa? What has she done now?"

The first voice answered with ill-disguised glee. It seems that for a certain type of woman, no matter her class, no matter her nationality, if she be a bearer of tidings—preferably bad—her day is made.

"My step-son's aunt has heard a strange tale. As you know, she is going to get married to that customs man who works down at the Western Gate. Her boy friend has been telling her that for months past Lady Rampa has been ordering all manner of things from India, and now the traders in their caravans are beginning to deliver the goods. Have you heard anything about it?"

'Well, I did hear that there was a special affair going to be held in their gardens in the near future, but you must remember that the Great Lord Rampa was our Regent when the Inmost One went to India during the invasion of the British that did so much harm. I suppose its only natural that one of the leading ladies of our country should want to order something. I don't see what she's doing wrong in that, do you?"

The informant exhaled gustily and then drew a deep breath and declaimed, "Ahh! But you don't know the whole of it, you don't even know the half of it! I've heard tell from one of my friends who serves one of the waiting-monks down at the Kesar—he comes from the Potala, you know—that a very very thorough horoscope and life reading is being prepared for that little fellow, you know, the little runt who's always getting into trouble and who seems to be such a sore trial to his father. I wondered if you had heard anything about that?"

The second lady thought a moment, and then she replied, "Yes, but you must remember that Paljör died recently—I saw his body being carried out with my very own eyes. The Body Breakers carried him out very reverently from the house, and the two priests accompanied him as far as the gate, but with my very own two eyes I saw that as soon as the two priests turned back the poor little body was unceremoniously dumped, belly down, on the back of a pony and was taken off to the Ragyab so that the Disposers of the Dead could break him up and feed him to the vultures. He had to be disposed of."

"No, no, no!" expostulated the exasperated informer, "you miss the whole point—you cannot have much experience of these social matters; with the death of the older boy that little fellow, Lobsang, is now the heir to the Lhalu family estates and fortunes, they are millionaires, you know. They've got money here, they've got money in India, and they've got money in China. I think they must be our wealthiest family. And this little fellow, why should he inherit it all? Why should he have such a life of luxury before him when we have to work—my husband said to me that, never mind, one of these days there will be a change, we shall take the residences of the upper parties and we shall live in luxury and they will work for us. We shall see what we shall see if we only live long enough, praise be the day."

There had been the sound of slow footsteps coming through the gloaming. Now a faint blur of face could be discerned and the black, black tresses of a Tibetan woman. "I could not help hearing what was said," the newcomer announced, "but we have to remember that this little lad, Lobsang Rampa, he's going to have a hard life ahead of him because all those with money have a very, very hard life indeed."

"Oh well then," replied the informer, "all of us should

have a very very easy time indeed. We've no money at all, have we?" With that she burst into cackles of witch-like laughter.

The newcomer went on, "Well, I've heard it said that a big affair is being planned so that the Great Lord Rampa can proclaim his son, Lobsang, to be his heir. I've heard, too, that the boy is going to be sent off to India to be trained, and the trouble then will be to keep him out of the hands of the British because the British are trying to get control of our country, you know, and look at the damage they've done. But, no, that boy, rich or poor, he's got a hard life ahead of him, you mark my words—you mark my words." The voices drifted off as the three women went carefully along the Lingkor Road, passing along by the Snake Temple, passing along by the Kaling Chu to cross the Chara Sanpa Bridge.

Just a few yards away—or perhaps a few yards more than that!— the subject of their discussion, a small boy not yet seven years of age, tossed restlessly on the hard hard floor of his room. He was asleep more or less, having fitful dreams, having also frightful nightmares; he was thinking of kites and how awful it would be if it was ever found out that he was the one who was flying the kite that swooped down on the travellers and scared their ponies so much that one of the riders fell off and rolled straight into the river, such an important man that rider was, too, as assistant to an Abbot of one of the Lamaseries. The poor boy turned and writhed in his sleep as in his dream-state he thought of all the dire punishments that would be inflicted upon his protesting body should he ever be revealed as the culprit.

Life was quite hard for young boys of the leading families in Lhasa. Those boys were supposed to set an example to others, they were supposed to endure hardship to toughen them for the battles of life, they were supposed to have greater hardship than those of lowly birth, to act as an example, to show that even the sons of the wealthy, even the sons of those who ruled the country, could endure pain, suffering, and privation. And the discipline for a boy not yet even seven years of age was something which Western boys of any age would never endure.

From beyond the Bridge there came the mumble, mumble of female voices as the three women stopped for a last chat before each departed to her own home. There came on errant breezes the words "Rampa," "Yasodhara," and then a mumble of voices until at last the gravel beneath their feet stirred restlessly as the women bade each other goodnight and went each her own respective way.

In the great Lhalu residence, whose massive front gate had so well withstood the assaults of the British infantry that they could gain access only by breaching the stone wall, the family were asleep, all except the "Guardians of the Night," those who stood watch and called out the night hours and the state of the weather so that any who by chance should be awake should know of the progress of the night.

Adjacent to the chapel of Lhalu residence were the Stewards' quarters. The highest class Tibetan officials maintained their own chapels in their residence staffed by one or two priests; the Rampa residence was of such importance that two priests were considered absolutely necessary. Every three years the priests—monks from the Potala—would be replaced by others so that those in household service should not become too effete through their domestic domicile. One of the lamas, for these monks were indeed lamas, had but recently joined the household. The other was soon to leave to return to the stern discipline of the lamasery, and the latter was tossing restlessly, wondering how he could prolong his stay for it was indeed the chance of a lifetime to see the heir of a great family have his horoscope proclaimed to the public so that all might know in advance what manner of man he would grow up to be.

This was a young lama, one who had come to the Lhalu estate with high recommendations from his Abbot, but he had proved to be a sorry disappointment. His amusements were not wholly ecclesiastical, not wholly priestly, for he was one of those who had that which is termed "the wan-

32

dering eye," and his glances strayed ever and again to the young and comely members of the domestic staff. The Steward who lived to the left of the chapel had noticed this and had registered a complaint, and so the poor young lama was facing dismissal in some disgrace. His successor had not yet been appointed and the young man was wondering how he could delay matters so that he could have the fame of being one of the participants in the celebrations and religious services to follow.

The poor wretched Steward, also, was having much distress. Lady Rampa was indeed a difficult woman, very harsh in her judgement at times, apt to condemn without giving a man a chance to explain that some of these difficulties were not of his making. Now he had goods on order for some three months, and—well, everyone knew how slow the Indian traders were—but Lady Rampa was making a terrible commotion and saying that the Steward was endangering the success of the whole enterprise by his inefficiency in getting supplies. "What can I do?" he muttered to himself as he tossed and turned on his blanket on the floor. "How can I persuade the dealers to bring the goods on time?" So muttering he rolled over on to his back, his mouth fell open, and he emitted such horrendous snores that one of the night watchmen looked in to see if he was dying!

Lady Rampa was turning restlessly too. She was very socially-conscious. She was wondering if the Steward was absolutely sure of the order of precedence, wondering if all the messages had been written, all the invitations on the special hand-made paper tied up with ribbon and then placed in a cleft stick which fast riders would carry mounted on their ponies. It had to be done just right, she thought, one could not have an inferior receiving an invitation before his superior had received one. These matters leak out, there are ever people anxious to pull down a hard working hostess who is trying to do the best for her family prestige. Lady Rampa twisted and turned, wondering about the food supplies, wondering if by any chance things would not arrive on time.

Nearby in a little room sister Yasodhara was fretting a bit. Her mother had already decreed what she would wear at the party and it wasn't at all what Yasodhara wanted to wear, she had different ideas altogether. After all, as she said to herself, this is the one time in the year to really look over the boys and see which one of them would be suitable as a husband in later years, and to look over the boys meant that she too must have something to attract them—clothing, it must be suitable clothing, her hair must be well brushed with yak butter, her clothes must be dusted with the finest of jasmine. She had to do everything possible to attract what she hoped would be a good husband for the future, but her mother—mothers never understood, they were of a bygone age, they didn't understand at all how young girls had to go along nowadays, they had forgotten such things. Yasodhara lay back and thought and thought, and planned could she add a ribbon here or a flower there, how could she improve her appearance?

As the night grew older and older and the new dawn, the dawn of a new day, was ready to be born the booming of conches and the blare of trumpets awakened the fitfully sleeping household. The youngest Rampa opened a sleep-bleared eye, grunted, and turned over again to be fast asleep before the turning motion was completed.

Down near the Steward's office the night watchmen were going off duty while a fresh shift were taking their places. The most menial of the servants awakened with a start at the blaring noises from the surrounding temples and jumped to their feet, struggling into half-frozen clothes. Theirs was the task of seeing that the smouldering fires were raked and stirred into fresh life, theirs was the task of polishing the rooms, cleaning the place, before "the family" got down to see it in its over-night state of untidiness.

In the stables where the many horses were kept, and in the farm buildings at the back where the yaks were housed servants rummaged around, scooping up the manure deposited there by the animals overnight. Dried and mixed with a few scraps of wood this would provide the staple fuel of Tibet.

The cooks reluctantly turned out to face another day, they were tired, they had been busy for several weeks past preparing food in fantastic quantities and having the additional task of trying to protect the food from the depredations of light-fingered small boys and light-fingered small girls, too. They were tired, they were sick of the whole affair, they were saying to each other, "Why doesn't this thing get started and finished so that we can have some peace again. The Mistress has gone off her head even worse with all the preparations."

The Mistress—the Lady Rampa—had indeed been busy. For days she had been in her husband's office plaguing his secretaries to provide lists of all the most important people living in Lhasa, and some chosen few from other nearby centres. As well she made the hard demand that suitable foreigners who could be of beneficent influence later be invited, but here again there was the question of protocol and the order of seniority, who came before whom, who would be insulted in THIS position when they felt that they should be in THAT position. It was all a great task, a great trial, a great tribulation, and the servants were tired of getting a list one day and finding that the next day a fresh list would supersede the one issued the day before.

For days now the whole place had been scoured, fine gritty sand had been used to shine up stonework mellowed by age, strong men servants with cloth around their feet and heavy blocks of stone wrapped in cloth trudged around the house pushing their heavy stone burden across floors that were already mirror-bright.

In the gardens weary gardeners on hands and knees went over the ground removing weeds, even removing little stones which were of the wrong colour. The mistress of the house was a hard task mistress indeed, this was the high point of her life, the son and heir of the Lhalu establishment, one who could be a prince or—what?—was to be launched and only the astrologers would tell what was to be his life, but the astrologers would give no hint, would give no forewarning of what their Reading would reveal.

The lady of the house, the wife of one of the most powerful men in lay-life of Tibet, hoped and hoped that her son would leave the country and be educated elsewhere, she hoped that she would be able to persuade her husband that she should make frequent visits to her son studying in a different country. She hoped to visit different countries, for long she had surreptitiously glanced at some of the magazines brought to Lhasa by itinerant traders. She had her plans, she had her dreams and her ambitions, but everything depended on the verdict of the Chief Astrologer and everyone knew how uncaring of one's social position astrologers could be.

Now the time was fast approaching when this great Party was to be held. Traders were entering by the Western Gate and making fast footsteps toward the Lhalu residence, the wiser ones—or those with greater business acumen—knew that the Lady Rampa would soon fall prey to their wiles if they could produce something new, something that hadn't been seen in Lhasa before, something which would make her neighbours and social competitors exclaim in feigned awe which really concealed frustration and jealousy that They had not had it first.

So many a trader made his slow way from the Western Gate along the Lingkor Road, around the back of the Potala, past the Snake Temple to the Lhalu residence, there to attempt to beguile the lady of the house with strange exotic items with which she could entertain and amaze her guests. Some took their yak trains and brought their whole stock-in-trade to the residence so that the lady in person could see precisely what they had to sell, and of course for such an important occasion the prices must be inflated because no lady who was indeed a lady would even dare to bargain or quibble at the prices asked for fear that the traders would mention to the neighbours that Lady Rampa could not pay the proper price but wanted a discount, or concessions, or samples.

Day after day the yak trains went by, day after day the

men from the stables scooped up the bounty from the yaks and added it to the pile of fuel which was so rapidly growing, and indeed much extra fuel would be needed for the cooking, for the heating, and for the bonfires, because who could possibly have a good party without a good bonfire?

The gardeners, having satisfactorily cleared the ground of all weeds, turned their attention to the trees, making sure that there were no broken branches, making sure that there were no dead branches which could appear unsightly and lead to an accusation of an ill-kept garden. Even more disastrous would be if some small branch fell upon some noble lady and disarranged her hairstyle which over hours would have been piled on a special lacquered wooden framework. So the gardeners were tired of parties, tired of work, and yet they dare not slack for the Lady Rampa seemed to have eyes everywhere, no sooner would a man sit down for a moment to rest an aching back than she would appear screaming with rage that he was delaying things.

At last the order of precedence was decided upon and approved by the Great Lord Rampa himself who personally affixed his seal to each of the invitations as they were carefully prepared by monk-scribes. The paper was specially made for the occasion, it was thick paper with a rough edge, almost a deckle-edge, in fact. Each sheet was roughly twelve inches wide by two feet long. These invitations did not follow the normal size or pattern as used in lamaseries; in lamaseries the paper is wider than it is long, but when there were very important invitations they were written on a narrower paper which was about twice as long as it was wide because after the invitation was accepted the paper would be fastened to two bamboo rods richly decorated at the ends, and then the invitation would be carefully suspended from a string and used as a decoration to show how important the recipient was.

The Lord Rampa was one of the Upper Ten families in Lhasa. The Lord Rampa himself was actually one of the Upper Five, but Lady Rampa was one of the Upper Ten, otherwise they could not have married. In view of the fact that each of them had such high social status two seals had to be affixed to the invitation, one for His Lordship and one for Her Ladyship, and then because they were married and had such an extensive estate they had a third seal which was known as the Estate Seal, and that too had to go upon the document. Each seal was of a different colour, and the Lady Rampa and the Steward were in a state bordering on frenzy lest the messengers were clumsy and did something which would crack the fragile, brittle seals.

Special message-sticks were prepared. These had to be of exactly the same length and very nearly the same thickness, each had a special slot at one end which would receive and hold the message. Then just below that slot there was a piece fixed on which bore the family coat of arms. Below the coat of arms there were narrow strands of a very tough paper on which were printed prayers, hoping for protection for the messenger and for a safe delivery of the messages, and hoping that the recipient would be able to accept the invitation.

For some time the messengers were carefully drilled in the most imposing manner to ride and deliver the messages. They sat upon their horses waving their message-sticks in the air as if they were spears, then on the signal they would charge forward and one by one would approach the Captain of the Guard who was drilling them. He, pretending to be the householder or the householder's steward, would graciously accept the message from the message-stick which was extended and inclined toward him. He would with great respect take the message and bow toward the messenger who was, after all, the representative of "the family." The messenger would bow back, would wheel his horse, and would gallop off from whence he came.

When all the messages, or invitations, were prepared they were placed in order of precedence, and the most imposing messenger took the most important message, and so on, and then off they galloped to deliver the invitations.

Other messengers would come forward, each take a message, and lodge it in the cleft of the stick and gallop off. Soon they would return and the whole procedure would be gone through again until, at long last, all the invitations had gone out, and now was the trying time when the Steward and the others had to sit back and wait and wait, and wonder how many would accept the invitations. Had they too much food? Had they not enough? It was most wearing to the nerves.

Some of the guests would be content to stay in the gardens, particularly if they were not of sufficient social status to be accepted into the house itself, but others—well, they were more important and they would have to enter the house, and the representatives of the clergy would also want to see the chapel. So all the lacquer was stripped from the altars and from the altar rails, and men worked with handfuls of cloth which were dipped in moist sand and scraped, and scraped, and scraped until the wood beneath the lacquer was bright and as new. Then a special priming coat was put on, and when that was dry lacquer, many layers of it, was most carefully painted on to the altars and the railings so that in the end the surface shone like the surface of still water on a sunny day.

The poor wretched servants were each called before the lady of the house and the Steward, and they were carefully inspected to see that their clothing was suitable and to see that everything was clean. If their clothing did not pass muster then it had to be carefully washed, for which purpose great cauldrons of hot water were prepared. At last, when the tension was reaching its height, all the invitations were answered, all the servants had been inspected, and all their special clothing had been put aside, not to be worn until The Day. So a tired household sat back in the late evening to await the dawn of a new day when Fate would be revealed.

Slowly the sun sank behind the Western mountains sending up a myriad of scintillating points of light from the ever-present spume blowing from the highest peaks; the snow glowed blood-red, and then darkened to blue, and on to purple. At last there was only the faint loom of the darkness of the sky and the glittering pin-points of light which were the stars.

At the Lhalu residence mysterious points of light appeared amid the well-kept trees. A chance traveller along the Lingkor Road slowed his step, hesitated, made as if to go on again, and then turned and walked back so that he could see what was afoot, or, more accurately, what was a-tree!

Excited voices came from the gardens, and the wayfarer just could not resist the temptation to pursue the matter further and to find out what it was that was causing such raised voices and what was, apparently, an altercation. As quietly as he could he shinned up the rough stone wall and rested his chest on the top with his arms supporting him, then he could see a novel sight indeed. There was the lady of the house, Lady Rampa, plump, short, almost square, in fact. At either side of her she had two tall servants, each carrying a lighted butter lamp and trying to shield the wavering flame so that it should not be extinguished and arouse Her Ladyship's ire.

Disgruntled gardeners moved disconsolately amid the trees fixing little butter lamps to certain of the lower branches, and then with flint and steel sparks ignited the tinder. Vigorous blowing produced a flame, and from the flame a piece of well-soaked-in-butter stick was used to transfer the flame to the butter lamps. The lady was not at all sure where she wanted the lamps, there was endless fumbling about in the darkness with the little flickering lights merely intensifying the purple night. At last there was a commotion and a very large figure came prancing out, shouting with rage: "You're ruining my trees, my trees, my trees—you're ruining my trees. I will not have this nonsense. Extinguish those lamps immediately!" The Lord Rampa was mighty proud of his wonderful trees, trees and gardens which were famed throughout Lhasa. He was indeed in a frenzy of excitement in case damage should have been caused to some of the newly budding flowers on the trees.

40

His wife, Her Ladyship, turned to him with lofty mien and said, "You are indeed making a spectacle of yourself, my lord, in front of the servants. Do you not think I am capable of managing this affair? It is my home as well as yours. Do not disturb me." The poor Lord snorted like a bull, one could almost imagine fire coming from his nostrils. He turned angrily on his foot, and hurried away back to the house, there was the sound of a door slamming, a sound so intense and heavy that any less substantial door would surely have been shattered with the shock.

"The incense brazier, Timon, the incense brazier. Are you altogether stupid man? Put it over there, never mind about lighting it now—put it over there." Poor Timon, one of the housemen, struggled along with a heavy brazier, but it was more than one brazier, there were several. The night grew darker and darker, and still the lady of the house wasn't satisfied. But at last the wind blew chill and the Moon appeared and cast a frosty light over the proceedings. The man peering over the wall chuckled to himself and dropped down to the road to continue his journey muttering to himself, "Well! well! If that is the price of being a noble, then glad I am indeed to be merely a humble trader." His footsteps died away in the darkness, and in the garden the butter lamps were extinguished one by one. The staff and the lady of the house departed. In the garden a night bird sniffed the strange unusual smell which came from one of the butter lamps, the wick of which was still smouldering, and flew off with a startled cry of protest.

In the house there was sudden commotion; the boy had disappeared, the heir to the estates, the young princeling —where was he now? He was not in his bed. There was panic. The mother thought he must have run away, being frightened by the severity of his father. The father thought he must have run away, being frightened by the anger of his mother, for that day nothing that the poor boy did was right. He had been in trouble the day long, first for getting dirty, then for tearing his clothes, then for not being where he should have been at a certain time, then for not being present punctually for meals; everything was wrong for him.

Servants were roused, the grounds were searched, butter lamps flared, and flint and tinder smoked. A procession of servants went around the gardens calling for the young Master, but without avail, he wasn't to be found. Sister Yasodhara was awakened to ask her if she could account for the movements of her brother, but—no—she wiped her bleary eyes with the back of her hand, lay down again and was asleep while she was still sitting.

Servants hurried down the road in the darkness to see if the boy had gone away. Other servants searched the house from top to bottom, and eventually in a storeroom Lobsang was found, asleep on a bag of grain with a cat at each side of him, and all three were snoring mightily. But not for long! The father rushed forward with a roar of rage which almost seemed to shatter the walls, certainly it made the dust from the grain bags jump and dance in the air. The lamps carried by servants flickered, and one or two went out. The poor boy was grasped tightly by the neck while one mighty hand lifted him up high. The mother rushed forward expostulating, "Stop! Stop! Be very sure you don't mark him because tomorrow he will be the cynosure of all the eyes of Lhasa. Just send him to bed." So the poor boy was given a hearty thump and pushed forward so violently that he fell on his face. One of the men servants picked him up and carried him away. Of the cats there was no sign.

But in the great Potala, at the level assigned to the Astrologers, the activity still continued. The Chief Astrologer was carefully checking his figures, carefully checking his charts, rehearsing what he was going to say, practising the intonation which he would find necessary. Around him lama-astrologers took each sheet of paper and with two other lamas checking every sheet was placed in its correct order, there could be no possibility of error here, no possibility of reading from the wrong page and bringing the College of Astrologers into disrepute. As each book was completed its wooden cover was placed on top and the book was held together with twice the customary number of tapes just so that everything would be doubly sure.

The monk assigned to be the personal attendant of the Chief Astrologer was carefully brushing his best robe, making sure that the zodiacal signs with which it was embellished were bright and fixed on securely. Then, as he was an old man, he used two sticks and those two sticks were carefully examined for any unsuspected flaws or cracks, after which they were passed to a polishing-monk who polished them until they shone like burnished copper.

From the temple areas the gongs boomed, the trumpets blared, and there was a susurration of scurrying feet as the religious monks went about their first night service. The astrological monks had been excused attendance because of the importance of the task allotted to them, because they could not risk dropping everything to go to service and then finding on the morrow that some error had crept in.

So at last the butter lamps were extinguished one by one. Soon there was no light except the light of the heavens, the starlight and the moonlight, but the starlight and the moonlight were augmented by the brilliant reflections from the lakes and rivers which traversed and criss-crossed the Plain of Lhasa. Every so often a dazzling sheet of water would cascade in a burst of glittering silver, like molten silver, as some great fish rushed up to the surface for a gulp of air.

All was silent except for the croaking of bull frogs and the cries of night birds in the distance. The Moon sailed in solitary splendour across the purple sky, the light of the stars dimmed as clouds from India obscured their glimmer. Night was upon the land, and all those except the creatures of the night slept.

CHAPTER THREE

The first faint light appeared over the jagged Eastern horizon. Great mountain ranges stood up in the starkest black and behind them the sky was becoming luminous.

On the topmost floor of the lamaseries monks and lamas stood ready to greet the new day, the topmost floor —the roof—in each case had a special platform or parapet on which great conches and trumpets some fifteen to twenty feet long stood on stands.

The Valley of Lhasa was a pool of inky black. The Moon had long since set, and the stars were diminished by the paling of the sky beyond the Eastern mountains. But the Valley of Lhasa still slept, still lived in the deepest darkness of night, not until the Sun lifted well above the mountains would the deep-lying lamaseries and houses welcome daylight.

Here and there dotted randomly throughout the Valley infrequent pinpoints of light appeared as a lama or a cook or a herdsman had to prepare for a very early start to his work. The faint, faint gleams served merely to accentuate the velvet blackness, so black that not even the trunk of a tree could be distinguished.

The light beyond the Eastern mountains increased. First there was a vivid flash of light, then a red beam shot up, followed immediately by what appeared to be an absolutely green shaft of light which was one of the features of the early morning sunrise and the late night sunset. Soon there came broader shafts of light, and within minutes there was a startling golden glow outlining the high peaks, showing the ever-present snow reflecting off high glaciers and projecting down into the Valley the first signs that the day had appeared. With the first appearance of the sun over the topmost edge of the mountains the lamas blew hard into their trumpets, and others sounded into the conches so that the very air seemed to shake with the sound. There was no immediate reaction to the noise, though, for the people of the Valley were well used to the sound of trumpets and conches and could ignore it just as people in cities can ignore the roaring of aircraft, the clattering of garbage collections, and all the rest of the noises of "civilisation."

Here and there, though, a sleepy night bird uttered a startled chirp before putting his head beneath his wing again and going off to sleep. Now was the time of the creatures of the day. Gradually the day birds came awake, cheeping sleepily and then flapping their wings to get rid of the stiffness of the night. Here and there a feather drifted down and was blown at the whim of the vagrant breeze.

In the waters of the Kyi Chu and at the Snake Temple fish were stirring lazily from their night time drifting near the surface. Fish in Tibet could always rise near the surface because Buddhists do not take life and there were no fishermen in Tibet.

The old man twisted at the sound of the bugles and the roaring of the conches, twisted and sleepily sat upright. From his low angle he peered upwards at the sky, and then a sudden thought struck him and he rose creakily to his feet. His bones were aged, his muscles tired, so he rose with circumspection and made his way to a window and looked out—looked out across the now-awakening City of Lhasa. Below him in the Village of Shö little lights were beginning to appear, one after another, as butter lamps were being lit so that official who were going to be busy this day would have ample time for their preparations.

The aged Astrologer shivered in the early dawn chill, and pulled his robe more tightly around him. Inevitably his thoughts turned to the Lhalu estate which could not be seen from his vantage point for he looked out over the Village of Shö and the City of Lhasa, and the Lhalu residence was at the other side of the Potala facing the wall

45

with the carved figures which was so much an attraction for wandering pilgrims.

The old man slowly lowered himself again to his blankets, and rested while he thought of the events of the day. This day, he thought, would be one of the high points of his career, perhaps the culminating point of his career. Already the old man could feel the hand of approaching death upon him, he could feel the slowing down of his body processes, he could feel that already his Silver Cord was thinning. But he was glad that there was yet one more function he could perform and bring credit to the office of Chief Astrologer of Tibet. So thinking he dozed off, to be awakened with something of a start as a lama bustled into the room exclaiming: "Honorable Astrologer, the Day is upon us, we have no time to lose, we have again to check the horoscope and the order in which the points are to be presented. I will assist you to rise, Honorable Astrologer." So saying, he bent down and put an arm around the shoulders of the old man and gently raised him to his feet.

By now the light was increasing rapidly, the sun was clear of the Eastern mountain range and was reflecting light to the Western side of the Valley; while those houses and lamaseries right beneath the Eastern range were yet in darkness, those on the opposite side were in almost full daylight.

The Potala was coming awake. There was the strange stir which humans always make when they are getting themselves into motion at the beginning of a day, there was a feeling of awareness that here were humans ready to continue the sometimes tedious business of living. Little silver bells were tinkling, every so often there would come the lowing of a conch or perhaps the brassy blare of a trumpet. The old Astrologer and the others around him were not aware of the clanking and turning of the Prayer Wheels, these were so much a part of their everyday existence that they had long since failed to perceive the noise the Prayer Wheels made, just as no longer did they notice the Prayer Flags which whipped to the morning breeze on the Potala heights above. Only a cessation of these noises would have been noticed by the startled people.

There was the scurry of feet along corridors, there was the moving of heavy doors. From somewhere came the chanting of psalm, religious psalm, psalms again welcoming the new day. But the old Astrologer had no time to notice things such as these for now there was the business of coming to full awareness and to attending to those functions which are so necessary after a night of sleep. Soon he would be having his morning meal of tsampa and tea, and then he would have to go and attend to the ritual of preparing for the Reading which·he was that day to give.

At the Lhalu family residence the servants were awake. Lady Rampa, too, was awake. And Lord Rampa, after a hasty breakfast, gladly mounted his horse and rode off with his attendants to the offices of the government in the Village of Shö. He was indeed glad to get away from his wife, get away from her bustling officiousness and her over-zealous approach to the events facing them. He had to make an early start to his work because later in the day it would be utterly incumbent upon him to return to play the part of the gracious host who was a Prince of Lhasa.

The heir to the Rampa estates was awakened and came to life most reluctantly. Today was "his" day, yet, he thought with some confusion, how could it be his day when Mother was planning to make such a social advantage from it. If he had his way he would forget the idea and disappear to the banks of the river so that he could watch the boatman ferrying people across the river, and perhaps when there were not many people to be ferried he could manage to con the ferryman into giving him free passage backwards and forwards, always with the excuse, of course, that he would help pole the ferry.

The poor wretched boy was most unhappy at the hard-hearted man servant who was thoroughly smearing his hair with yak butter, and then plaiting a tight pig-tail with a curious twist in it. The yak butter was kneaded into the pig-tail until the latter was almost as stiff as a willow rod.

At about ten in the morning there was the sound and clatter of horses and a party of men rode in to the courtyard. The Lord Rampa and his attendants had returned from the government offices because it was necessary that the family should go to the Cathedral of Lhasa to give thanks for whatever mysteries were to be revealed on this day and, of course, to show to priests ever ready to believe that "blackheads" were irreligious that these were specially religious "black heads." In Tibet monks have shaven heads, while the ordinary people, the laity, had long hair, most times it was black hair, and because of the black hair they were referred to as "black heads."

People were waiting in the courtyard, Lady Rampa already upon a pony, and her daughter Yasodhara. At the last moment the heir of the family was grabbed and unceremoniously hoisted upon a pony who appeared equally reluctant. The gates were again opened and the party rode out with the Lord Rampa at the head. For about thirty minutes they rode in strange silence until at last they came to the small houses and the shops which surrounded the Cathedral of Lhasa, the Cathedral which had stood there for so many hundreds of years to afford a place of worship for the pious. The original stone floors were deeply grooved and scored by the footsteps of pilgrims and sightseers. All along the entrance to the Cathedral were lines of Prayer Wheels—big things indeed—and as each person went by they turned the Wheel as was the custom so that a most curious tinkling clatter was set up which had an almost hypnotic effect.

The inside of the Cathedral was heavy—overpowering in its heaviness—with the scent of incense and the memory of incense which had been burned during the past thirteen or fourteen hundred years. The heavy black beams of the roof seemed to have clouds of incense growing from them, bluish smoke, grey smoke, and occasionally a smoke of a brownish hue.

There were various Gods and Goddesses represented in

golden figures, wooden figures, and porcelain figures, and before each were the offerings of pilgrims. Every so often the offerings would be swept behind a metal net to protect them from pilgrims whose piety was overcome by the desire to participate in the wealth of the Gods.

Heavy candles burned and made flickering shadows throughout the dim building. It was a sobering thought even to a small boy not yet seven years of age to reflect that these candles had been kept alight by pouring on butter throughout thirteen or fourteen hundred years. The poor boy gazing wide-eyed around him thought, "Let's get this day over and perhaps I shall be able to go to some other country, away from all this holiness." Little did he know what was in store for him!

A big cat strolled lethargically forward and rubbed against the legs of the heir of the Rampa family. The boy stooped and dropped to his knees to fondle the big cat who roared with delight. These were the guardian cats of the temple, astute students of human nature who could tell at a glance those who would be likely to attempt to steal and those who could be trusted. Normally such cats would never, never approach anyone other than their own particular keeper. For a moment there was stunned silence among the onlookers, and some of the monks faltered in their chanting as their eyes wandered to the sight of the boy on his knees by the big cat. The picture was soon spoiled, however, because the Lord Rampa, his face suffused with rage, bent down and picked up the boy by the scruff of his neck, shook him like a housewife shaking out a duster, gave him a slap on the ear which made the boy think there was a thunderstorm, and then dumped him on his feet again. The cat turned toward His Lordship and uttered a very long, loud hiss, and then turned with dignity and strode away.

But the time had come to return to the Lhalu residence for soon the guests would start arriving. Many of the guests came early so that they could get the pick of what was offered, and the pick of what was offered included the best place in the garden. So the party left the confines of

49

the Cathedral and went out into the street again. The boy raised his eyes and saw the flags fluttering over the road which led to India, and he thought, "Shall I soon be on that road going to another country? I shall soon know, I suppose, but, my goodness, I would like something to eat!"

The party rode on retracing their footsteps, and after twenty-five to thirty minutes they were again entering the courtyard of the house where they were greeted by an anxious Steward who thought that there might have been some delay and that he would have to explain to irate guests that the host and hostess had been unaccountably delayed at the Cathedral.

There was time for a hurried meal, and then the heir to the estates rushed to the window at unexpected noises approaching up the road. Monk-musicians were arriving, their musical instruments were clattering as they rode along the road on their ponies. Every so often a monk would give an experimental blow to his trumpet or clarinet to make sure that it was in tune. Now and again a monk would give a hearty bonk to a drum to make sure that the skin was at the correct tautness. Eventually they entered the courtyard and went by the side path into the gardens, carefully depositing their instruments on the ground. The instruments deposited, they reached for the Tibetan beer gladly. The beer was there in some profusion to prepare them—to get them in the right mood to make jovial music instead of sombre classical stuff.

But there was no time to deal with the musicians, the first of the guests were arriving. They came in a body. It seemed as if all Lhasa was moving on to the Lhalu residence. Here came a small army of men on horseback, all heavily armed, it was something like the invading army sent by the British, but this army was armed only because ceremony and protocal demanded it. They rode with men on the outside, and between the lines of men the women rode where they were adequately protected from any imaginary attack. The armed servitors had their spears and pikes gaily decorated with flags and with pennants. Here and there, as a monk was in the party, Prayer Flags fluttered from a staff.

In the courtyard itself there were two lines of servants, headed by the Steward on one side and the Chief Household Priest on the other. There was much ado with bowing, returning bows, and bowing again as the guests were ushered in. Each guest was helped off his horse as if—as the heir to the household thought—they were all a lot of paralysed dummies. Their horses were led away and given ample food. Then, depending upon the status of the guests, they were either shown into the garden and left to fend for themselves, or shown into the house where they would exclaim over this or that article, articles which had been put out especially to impress the guests! Of course, in Tibet scarves are given and received, and there was much confusion as the arriving guests presented scarves and then received scarves in return. Sometimes there was a most awkward incident when some bemused servant would unthinkingly hand back to the guest the scarf which he or she had just presented, there would be embarrassed smiles and muttered apologies, but soon the matter would be straightened out.

Lady Rampa was red of face and perspiring freely. She was terrified that the old Astrologer—the Chief Astrologer of all Tibet—must have died, or fallen into the river, or been trampled upon by a horse, or some similar mishap because there was no sign of him, and the purpose of the whole party was to have the Reading of the future for the heir to the household. Without the Chief Astrologer that could not be done.

A servant was despatched at the run to ascend to the highest point in the house and to look out toward Potala, to see if there was any sign of the approaching cavalcade which would herald the impending arrival of the Astrologer. The servant departed and soon was seen on the topmost roof, he was gesticulating with his arms, and dancing a little jig in his excitement.

Lady Rampa was furious, absolutely frustrated, she had no idea what the servant was trying to convey, it looked as if he were drunk more than anything else. So hastily she sent a fresh servant to get a report as to what was happening. Soon the two servants arrived together and explained that the Astrological cavalcade was just crossing the Plain of Kyi Chu. That was the signal for increased fervour. Lady Rampa ushered everyone out of the house and into the garden, telling them to take their places because the great Chief Astrologer was arriving any moment. The monk-musicians straightened up and started to play, making the air shake and vibrate with the excitement that they put into the event.

The Lhalu estate gardens were large and very well kept. There were trees from all over Tibet, even some from India, from Bhutan and Sikkim. Bushes, too, grew in great profusion with exotic blooms entrancing the eye. But now the wonderful showpiece of a garden was thronged with avid sightseers, people who had no thought for horticulture, people who were there for SENSATION. The Great Lord Rampa wandered disconsolately about, chewing on his knuckles with an agony of anguished frustration and at the same time trying to smile amiably at those people whom he felt he should beam upon.

Lady Rampa was almost wearing herself shorter by the amount of running about she was doing; she was in a continual bustle, trying to see the Lord Rampa wasn't too austere, trying to see what the heir to the estate was doing, what the servants were doing—and keeping a ready eye for the arrival of the Chief Astrologer.

There came the sound of horses' steps. The Steward hurried to the main gate which was carefully shut behind him. He stood ready to order its opening at just the right moment to make the maximum effect.

Guests had heard the horses and were now streaming from the garden into a very large room which, for the occasion, had been converted into a refectory-reception room. Here they found buttered tea waiting for them and, of course, delicacies from India, very sweet sticky cakes which would effectively glue them up and prevent them from talking so much!

There came the sound of a deep-toned gong, its voice echoing and reverberating around the building, a mighty gong some five feet high and which was only used on the most solemn occasions. Now a highly placed man servant was standing by it giving it the special strokes which he had been practising on a smaller gong for days past.

The gong boomed, the gate swung open, and into the courtyard wheeled a cavalcade of young monks, lamas, and the Chief Astrologer. He was an old man, wizened, small, some eighty years of age. Close beside him, almost leg to leg, in fact, rode two lamas whose sole duty it was to make sure that the aged man did not topple off and get trampled underfoot.

The horses came to a stop, knowing full well that the end of the journey had come and now they would be well fed. The two lama-attendants jumped off their horses and carefully lifted the old Astrologer. Then the Lord Rampa came forward and there was the customary exchange of scarves, the customary bowing, and bowing in return. Then the Chief Astrologer and the Lord Rampa entered the reception room where all the assembled people bowed to him.

For a few moments there was a certain amount of confusion and turmoil. Then the Chief Astrologer, having politely tasted the proffered buttered tea, motioned to two lamas who carried the notes and charts.

The deep-toned gong sounded again, boom, boom, boom—boom. The far end of the reception room was flung open and the Chief Astrologer and his two lama-attendants walked forward through the door, out into the garden to where a great marquee—especially imported from India—had been erected. One side of the marquee was open so that the maximum number of people should be able to see and hear what was going on. Inside the marquee of dais had been erected with rails on three sides and near the front were four seats.

The Chief Astrologer and his two lama-attendants approached the dais and then four servants appeared carrying upright poles, or flambeau, because at the distal end there were large flares showing that these men were recognising that here in this marquee there were the flames of knowledge.

Four trumpeters next appeared. They sounded a fanfare. They were to draw attention to Lord and Lady Rampa because their son, the heir to the Lhalu estate, was the cause of all the "commotion," as one onlooker said. The Lord and Lady slowly mounted the dais, and stood behind the four chairs.

From another direction, and with their own retinue, there came two very very old men from the Lamasery of the State Oracle. These two old men from the Lamasery of Nechung were, after the Chief Astrologer, the most experienced astrologers in the country, they were collaborators with the Chief Astrologer, they had gone over the figures and charts and computations, and each of the sheets of the horoscope contained the seals of approval of each of these men.

The Chief Astrologer stood. The others sat. Suddenly there fell a hush upon the assembled company. The Chief Astrologer gazed out at the throng, and built up suspense by remaining quite silent for some moments, then at a gesture the two lamas moved forward, one to each side of him. The one on the right held the assembled book of the horoscope, the one on the left carefully removed the top wooden plaque, and the Chief Astrologer read his remarks.

People had to strain because, with age, the Astrologer had a thin, high voice which to those in the background blended with the birds who chirped in the topmost branches.

His opening remarks were the ritual remarks on such occasions; "Gods, devils, and men all behave in the same way," he said, "so the future can be foretold, but the future is not immutable. The Future can, within certain limits, be changed. Thus it is we can forecast only the probabilities, and having forecast the probabilities, predicted the good and the bad, then indeed we must leave the rest to those whose horoscopes we are reading." He stopped and looked about him, and the lama on the left removed the top sheet, leaving the second one exposed. The Astrologer took a deep breath and continued, "Here we have the most remarkable horoscope that the three of us have ever computed." He turned and bowed slightly to his two collaborators. Then, clearing his throat, he continued, "This is the horoscope of a young boy just six years of age. It is the most difficult horoscope and the hardest Life which we have encountered."

Lord and Lady Rampa shifted uneasily. Certainly this wasn't turning out as they expected, they weren't at all happy. But, with the training of their caste, they maintained an inscrutable expression. Behind them the cause of all the trouble, the heir to the estate, Lobsang Rampa, felt gloomy indeed. All this waste of time. How many people would have been crossing the river? What was the boatman doing? Were the cats all right? He felt he had to stand there like a stuffed dummy while three ancient, almost fossilised men decided what he would have to do with his life. Surely, he thought, he should have some say in what he was going to do. People had been telling him how wonderful it was to be the heir to such an immense estate, saying what a credit he could be to his parents. Well, he thought, he wanted to be a ferryman, he wanted to look after cats somewhere; certainly he didn't want to work.

But the Astrologer was droning on, and there was a complete silence from the audience, they were indeed enthralled. "This boy must go to the Medical Lamasery at Chakpori, he must do his penance and his homage before he can be permitted to enter, and having entered he must start as the lowest of the low and work his way up. He must learn all the Medical arts of Tibet, he must for a time do that which is almost unmentionable; he must work with the Disposers of the Dead that, in cutting up bodies, he may understand the structure of the human body. Having done this he will return to Chakpori, and study yet again. He will be shown the innermost mysteries of our land, of our Belief, and of our Science."

The old man held out his hand, and an attendant

quickly gave him a small silver beaker containing some liquid which he looked at and then swallowed. The attendant carefully took back the silver beaker and refilled it ready for the next demand.

The Astrologer went on: "Then shall come the time when no longer may he remain in this land of ours, instead he must journey to China to study medicine according to the Western style, for there is a Western School of Medicine in Chungking. At that School of Medicine he shall take a fresh name for let it not be known that the heir to Lhalu's shall be dealing with the bodies. Later he shall learn something which is quite incomprehensible to us at present, it is something which has not yet come about, something which is not yet properly invented. To our experienced brains it seems that he may do something which entails flying through the air, yet which is not the levitation which some of us can do here in Lhasa. So upon this particular aspect I must be obscure because indeed it is most obscure to the three of us. The boy, who then will be a young man, will have to work this out for himself, he will fly through the air by some means. Our pictures show something like the kites with which we are familiar, but this particular kite is not tethered to the ground by rope, instead it appears to be controllled by those who ride on it."

There was much muttering and urgent whispering from the congregation. This was wonders piled on wonders, never before had such things been spoken of. For a moment there was the uneasy shuffling of feet, and then the Astrologer took another drink and turned back to the, by now, diminishing sheets of paper.

"He shall have immense suffering, immense hardship, he shall enter a war against evil forces, he shall for some years be confined and undergo suffering such as few have undergone, the purpose of which will be to purify and to drive away the dross of any sensuality, and to build the power of the brain to endure. Later he shall get away from his captors after some immense explosion which throws a whole country, or a whole world, maybe, into confusion.

56

He shall travel by means which we cannot identify across a vast continent, and at the end of that travel he shall again be incarcerated unjustly, suffering will come upon him there with at least as great measure as it did in the other confinement. At last, by the intervention of unknown people, he shall be released and forced out of that great continent. He shall wander into many countries, meeting many people, seeing many cultures, learning many things. And then at last he shall go to a country where once again he shall not be welcomed because of his difference. The suffering will have changed him enormously so that he no longer seems of our own kind, but different. And when humans meet anything which is different they fear that thing, and that which they fear they hate and try to destroy."

The old man was looking tired. At last the senior attendant stepped forward, muttered to the Astrologer, and then said, "We will have a few minutes rest while our Chief Astrologer recuperates for the second half of this Reading. Let us, then, for the moment concentrate upon that which has been said so that we may the more easily assimilate that which is to follow." The Chief Astrologer sat down, refreshments were brought to him, and he watched the throngs of people. And as he sat watching the throngs of people he thought of his boyhood, he thought of the times he had climbed the high mountains in the deepest of the night so he could gaze upon the stars arrayed in the Heavens above. He had pondered long upon the significance of those stars, did they have influence on people? He decided to find out. By various means, and probably because he was fated to do so, he entered the Lamasery of the State Oracle and he was found to have quite abnormal ability at Astrology, an Astrology, of course, which is far superior to that of the Western world, far more complete and far, far more accurate. It includes more variables and could be projected at greater depth. The young man who was destined to be the Chief Astrologer of the whole of Tibet progressed rapidly, studying, studying, studying. He obtained the ancient texts of India,

57

the texts of China, and almost re-wrote the Science of Astrology in Tibet. As his skill rose his fame increased so that he was called upon by the heads of all the great houses of Lhasa, and then of other cities of Tibet. Soon he was called upon to do predictions for the government and for the Great Thirteenth himself. Always he was strictly honest. If he did not know, he said he did not know. He had predicted the British invasion, he had predicted the departure of the Great Thirteenth to another country, and his safe return, and he had made the prediction that there would be no real Dalai Lama after the Thirteenth had gone to the state of transition; there would be another but he would have been selected as a matter of political expediency in an attempt to assuage the territorial ambitions of the Chinese. He had made the prediction that in sixty years, or, so, there would be the end of Tibet as it was then known, a completely fresh order would come into force which would cause extreme hardship and suffering, but might, if it were handled correctly, have the effect of sweeping away an out-moded system and bringing, after a hundred years or so, benefits to Tibet.

The Chief Astrologer sipped his buttered tea and looked at the people before him. He watched the way some of the young men looked at the young women, and the way in which the young women glanced back, coyly, invitingly. He thought of his long years as a celibate monk, nearly eighty years, he thought, and he hardly knew in which way a woman differed from a man. His knowledge was of the stars, of the influence of the stars, and of men and women as they were affected by the stars. He looked at comely young women and wondered if it really was right for monks to be celibate. Surely, he thought, mankind should consist of two parts, the male and the female principle, and unless the two parts are united there cannot be a complete Man. He thought of all the tales he had heard of how women were becoming more and more arrogant, more trying to rule. He looked about at some of the older women with their harsh faces, and he noted their domineering attitude. And then he thought, well, perhaps it is that the time is not yet ripe for man and woman to be united to form one whole, to form one complete entity. But that will come, although not until the end of this Round of existence. So thinking, he gave up his cup to an attendant, and signalled that he was ready to continue.

A hush again fell upon the assembly, people were looking up toward the dais. As the old man was assisted to his feet the books were again placed before him. He looked around once more, and said, "Some of the experiences which will befall the subject of this Reading are so far beyond our own experiencce that they cannot be predicted in a sufficiently accurate form to be worthwhile. It is known definitely that this person has a great, great Task to do, it is a Task which is of the utmost importance to the whole of humanity, not of Tibet alone. It is known that there are evil forces, very evil forces indeed, who are working hard to negate that which he must do.

"He will encounter hatred, he will encounter every form of hardship and suffering, he will know what it is to be at the point of death and have to undergo the ordeal of transmigration into another body so that the work may go forward. But here in this other body fresh problems will arise. He will be disowned by his own people because of that political expediency which I have already mentioned. It will be considered to the benefit of a people as a whole that he be disowned, that he be not supported by those who should support him, by those who could support him, and I say again that these are probabilities because it is quite possible for our own people to support him and give him an opportunity to speak before the nations of the world so that, first, Tibet may be saved, and secondly, that great Task whose exact nature may not be mentioned may be the more speedily accomplished. But weak people in temporary abridged authority shall not be strong enough to assist him and so he shall battle alone against the forces of evil, and against the uncaring people whom he is trying to help."

The old man looked around and motioned to the left-hand attendant to remove the next sheet. The attendant blushed a little at having to be reminded, and speedily did as he was bade. The Astrologer went on: "There is a special association or group which gives information to peoples of the world beyond our confines. They are of insufficient spiritual stature to understand the Task which has to be accomplished, and their sensational hatred shall make the Task immeasurably more difficult. As well as this there is a small group of people who will be filled with burning hatred and will do everything possible to ruin the subject of this horoscope and cause him every distress."

The old man paused and put his hand on the topmost sheet as a signal that he had finished with the books. Then he turned and addressed the congregation, "With the years of my experience I say to you this; no matter how great the struggle, no matter how severe the suffering, the Task is worthwhile. The only battle that matters is the final battle. It does not matter who wins or who loses, the wars that continue until the final battle, and in the end the final battle shall be won by the powers of good, and that which has to be done shall be done." He bowed three times to the people, and then turned and bowed three times to the Lord and Lady Rampa. Then he sat down to rest his legs which were shaking with the weight of years.

The audience, whispering among themselves, quickly dispersed and went into the gardens in search of entertainment, and there was much entertainment offered—music, acrobats, jugglers, and, of course, food and drink. After the Astrologer and his two collaborators had rested awhile they rose and went into the great house where they had more to say to the parents of Lobsang Rampa. They had more to say to Lobsang as well, to say privately, alone with him.

Soon the Chief Astrologer departed on his way back to the Potala, and his two collaborators departed on their journey to the Lamasery of the State Oracle.

The day wore on. There came the dusk, and at the warning of dusk the assembled people wended their way out of the great gate and along the roads so they may reach their own homes before night and the perils thereof came upon them.

The darkness fell and out in the road beyond the great gate a lonely little boy stood looking down the road at the last of the departing guests and the carousing which they were making. He stood with hands clasped, thinking of a life of misery which had been predicted, thinking of the horrors of war which he did not understand, thinking of the insensate persecution yet to come. He stood there alone, alone in all the world, and no one had such a problem. He stood there and the night grew darker, and no one came to seek him and to lead him back. At last, as the Moon was full above, he lay down by the side of the road—the gate was shut anyhow—and in minutes there came a purring beside his head and a great big cat lay down beside him. The boy put his arms around the cat, the cat purred louder. Soon the boy drifted off to a troubled sleep, but the cat was alert, watching, guarding.

So ends the First Book,
the Book of As It Was In The Beginning.

BOOK TWO

The First Era.

CHAPTER FOUR

"Oh Lobsang, Lobsang," quoth Mother, her face pale with anger. "You have brought us absolute disgrace, I am ashamed of you. Your Father is ashamed of you, he is so angry with you that he has gone to the office and will be there all day, that has upset all my engagements, and its all you, Lobsang!" So saying she turned abruptly and hurried off as if she couldn't bear to look at me any longer.

Ashamed of me? Why should she be ashamed of me? I didn't want to be a monk, I didn't want all the horrible things predicted for me. Anyone with a grain of sense would know that. The predictions of yesterday had filled me with horror. It had been like the ice devils trailing their fingers up and down my spine. So she was ashamed of me, was she?

Old Tzu hove into sight almost like a moving mountain, he was so large. He looked at me and said, "Well, young man, you're going to have a rough life, aren't you? I think you'll make it. If you could not have stood all the strains and temptations you would not have been chosen for such a task. The craftsman chooses his tools according to the task to be done. Perhaps—who knows?—the craftsman who chose you to be his instrument may have chosen better than he knew." I looked at old Tzu somewhat cheered, but only "somewhat," and then I said, "But, Tzu, how have I disgraced Mother, how have I disgraced Father? I haven't done anything. I didn't want to become a monk. I just don't understand what they mean. Everyone today seems to be full of hate for me. My sister won't speak to me, my Mother reviles me, and my Father won't even stay in the house with me, and I don't know why."

Old Tzu painfully lowered himself to sit cross-legged on the floor, his wounds inflicted by the British were sorely troubling him. He had had damage to a hip bone and now—well—he had pain all the time. But he sat on the floor and talked to me.

"Your Mother," he said, "is a woman of great social ambition. She thought that as a son of a Prince of Tibet, later to be a Prince in your own right, you would have gone to a big city in India and there you would have learned much of the affairs of the world. Your Mother thought that you would be a social asset to her, she thought that if you went to India and perhaps to other countries, then she also could have gone on visits, and that for years, even before your birth, has been her all-consuming ambition. Now you have been chosen for a special Task, but that's not what she wanted, its not what your Father wanted. They wanted a shining figure in the political arena, a socialite, not a monk who is going to have to struggle all his life, not a man who would wander the face of the Earth like a pariah, shunned by his fellows for telling the truth, ostracised by those around him because he was trying to do a Task at which others have failed." Old Tzu snorted loudly.

All this seemed too utterly strange for belief. Why should I be penalised, victimised, for something I hadn't done and something I didn't want to do? All I wanted was to hang around the banks of the river and watch the ferrymen with their skin boats poling their way across the waters. All I wanted was to practise with my stilts and to fly my kites. But now—well, I just did not know what to make of things, I did not know why it had to be ME.

The days sped all too quickly, and at last as foretold I had to leave my home and go up the hill to the Chakpori Lamasery. There I had to undergo the ordeal of waiting, waiting outside the cynosure of all eyes. Small boys clustered around me as I sat cross-legged in the dust outside the great gates. The days were unendurably long, but I endured. The nights were unbearably tedious, but I bore them until at last that ordeal ended. I was admitted to the Lamasery as the lowest of the low, a new boy, one who was fair game, one who was there to be picked on, who

66

could have any manner of joke played upon him. The lowest of the low.

Time crawled, and I was homesick. I missed my home, I missed Tzu, I missed my sister Yasodhara; for the Mother who now had no love for me—well, I had strange sensations about her. Frankly, I missed her. Even more frankly, I felt guilty. How had I failed? Why were they so disappointed with me? How could I help that an astrologer had said I should go and suffer this and endure that? It wasn't my choice, no one in their right senses, I thought, would pick such a load of trouble as that which had been allocated to me.

I thought of my Father the last time I saw him before leaving home. He looked at me frozen-faced, he spoke to me harshly as if I were a stranger now, no longer with a home of my own, and no longer with parents of my own. He treated me more severely than he would have treated a convict who came to the door begging for food. He told me that I had disgraced the family by having such a kharma that I had to be a monk, a lama, a wanderer, one who would be mocked, sneered at and disbelieved.

Yasodhara—well, I just didn't know what to make of her attitude. She changed. We used to play together like any normal brother and sister, we used to get on passably well, just, in fact, like normal brothers and sisters do get on "passably well." But now she gave me such strange glances as if I were a stray dog that had crept in to the house and left an unwanted gift in some corner. The servants no longer showed me respect, the respect due to the heir of the Lhalu estates. To them I was just something which was lodged there for a few days until the seventh birthdate should come. Then on the seventh birthdate I would wander off alone without a word of goodbye from anyone, up the long and lonely path leading toward a career which I would not have wished upon my worst enemies.

At Chakpori there was the constant reek of drying herbs, the constant swish of herbal tea. Here much time was devoted to the herbalist code, and less time to religious disciplines. But we had very good tutors, all of them elderly men, some in fact had even been as far away as India.

I remember one elderly monk, or I should say lama, who was giving us a lecture, and then he got on to the subject of transmigration. "In the days of long ago," he said, "in fact long before recorded history began, giants walked upon the Earth. They were the Gardeners of the Earth, those who came here to supervise the development of life on this planet, because we are not the first Round of Existence here, you know, but like gardeners clearing a plot of land all life had been removed and then we, the human race, had been left here to make our own way, to make our own development." He stopped and looked around to see if his pupils were at all interested in the subject which he was propounding. To his gratified astonishment he found that people were indeed deeply interested in his remarks.

"The Race of Giants," he went on, "were not very suitable for life on Earth, and so by magical means the Race of Giants shrank until they were the same size as humans, thus they were able to mingle with humans without being recognised as the Gardeners. But it was often necessary for a different senior Gardener to come and carry out special tasks, it took too long to have a boy born to a woman and then wait out the years of his babyhood and childhood and teenage. So the science of the Gardeners of the Earth had a different system; they grew certain bodies and made sure that those bodies would be compatible with the spirit who would later inhabit them."

A boy sitting in the front suddenly spoke up: "How could a spirit inhabit another person?" The lama teacher smiled upon him and said, "I was just about to tell you. But the Gardeners of the Earth permitted certain men and women to mate so that a child was born to each, and the growth of that child would be most carefully supervised throughout, perhaps, the first fifteen or twenty or thirty years of life. Then there would come a time when a highly placed Gardener would need to come to Earth within a matter of hours, so helpers would place the trained body into a trance, into stasis, or, if you like, into a state of suspended animation. Helpers in the astral world would come to the living body together with the entity who wanted to go to Earth, with their special knowledge they could detach the Silver Cord and connect in its place the Silver Cord of the entity who was the Gardener of the Earth coming to the Earth. The host would then become the vehicle of the Gardener of the Earth, and the astral body of the host would go away to the astral world just as he would do in the case of a person who had died.

"This is called transmigration, the migration of one entity into the body of another. The body taken over is known as the host, and it has been known throughout history, it was practised extensively in Egypt and it gave rise to what is known as embalming because in those days in Egypt there were quite a number of bodies kept in a state of suspended animation, they were living but unmoving, they were ready for occupancy by higher entities just as we keep ponies waiting for a monk or lama to mount the animal and ride off somewhere."

"Oh my!" exclaimed one boy, "I expect friends of the host were mightily surprised when the body awakened and the one they had thought of as their friend in the past was possessed of all knowledge. My! I wouldn't like to be a host, it must be a terrible feeling to have someone else take over one's body."

The teacher laughed and said, "It would certainly be a unique experience. People still do it. Bodies are still prepared, specially raised so that if the need arises a different entity can take over a fresh body if it becomes necessary for the good of the world as a whole."

For days after the boys had discussed it, and in the way of boys some of them pretended that they were going to be taking over bodies. But to me, thinking back on that dread prediction, it was no joke, it wasn't amusing to me, it was an ordeal to even think about it. It was a continual shock to my system, so great a shock that at times I thought I would go insane.

One tutor in particular was intrigued by my love of cats, and the cats' obvious love for me. The tutor knew full well that cats and I conversed telepathically. One day after school hours he was in a very good mood indeed, and he saw me lying on the ground with four or five of our temple cats sitting on me. He laughed at the sight and bade me accompany him to his room, which I did with some apprehension because in those days a summons to a lama's quarters usually meant a reprimand for something done or not done, or extra tasks to be accomplished. So I followed him at a respectful distance, and once in his rooms he told me to sit down while he talked to me about cats.

"Cats," he said, "are now small creatures, and they cannot speak in the human tongue but only by telepathy. Many, many years ago, before this particular Round of Existence, cats populated the Earth. They were bigger, they were almost as big as our ponies, they talked to each other, they could do things with their forepaws, which then they called hands. They engaged in horticulture and they were largely vegetarian cats. They lived among the trees and their houses were in the great trees. Some of the trees were very different from those we now know upon the Earth, some of them, in fact, had great hollows in them like caves, and in those hollows, or caves, the cats made their homes. They were warm, they were protected by the living entity of the tree, and altogether they were a very congenial community. But one cannot have perfection with any species because unless there is some competition, unless there is some dissatisfaction to spur one on, then the creature having such euphoria degenerates."

He smiled at the cats who had followed me and who were now sitting around me, and then he went on, "Such happened to our brothers and sisters Cat. They were too happy, too contented, they had nothing to spur their ambition, nothing to drive them on to greater heights. They had no thought except that they were happy. They were like those poor people we saw recently who were bereft of sanity, they were content just to lie beneath the trees and let the affairs of the day take care of themselves. They

70

were static, and so being static they were a failure. As such the Gardeners of the Earth rooted them out as though they were weeds and the earth was allowed to lie fallow for a time. And in the course of time the Earth had reached such a stage of ripeness that again it could be re-stocked with a different type of entity. But the cats—well, their fault had been that they had done nothing, neither good nor bad. They had existed and that alone—existed. And so they were sent down again as small creatures like those we see here, they were sent to learn a lesson, they were sent with the inner knowledge that THEY had once been the dominant species, so they were reserved, very careful to whom they gave their friendship. They were sent to do a task, the task of watching humans and reporting the progress or the failures of humans so that when the next Round came much information would have been provided by cats. Cats can go anywhere, they can see anything, they can hear anything, and, not being able to tell a lie, they would record everything precisely as it occurred."

I know that I was quite frightened for the time being! I wondered what the cats were reporting about me. But then one old tom, a champion of many a fight, gave a "Rrrr" and jumped on my shoulders and butted his head against mine, so I knew everything was all right and they would not report me too badly.

Sometime after I lay upon my face on my blanket on the floor of the Infirmary because I had been very badly burned at the top of my left leg, the scars are with me yet, and the disfunction occasioned by the burn is one from which I still suffer. I was lying upon my face because I couldn't lie upon my back, and a well-loved lama entered and said, "Later, Lobsang, when you are healed and mobile I am going to take you to a certain peak in the mountains. I have there something to show you because, you know, the Earth has undergone many changes, the Earth has changed, the seas have altered, the mountains have grown. I am going to show you things which not more than ten people in the whole of Tibet have seen during the

71

past hundred years. So hurry up and get better, hurry up and heal, you have something of interest before you."

It was some months later when my Guide, the Lama Mingyar Dondup, who meant so much to me and who was more than mother and father and brother to me, led me along a path. He went a few feet ahead on a strong horse, and I rode behind him on a pony who was as wary of me as I was of him. He recognised me as a bad rider and I recognised him as a horse who recognised a bad rider. We had what in later years I would have called an armed neutrality, a sort of—well, if you don't do anything I won't either, we've got to live together somehow. But we rode on, and at long last my Guide stopped. I leaned over and slithered sideways off the pony. The trail ropes were dropped and the horse and pony would not then wander away, they were too well-trained.

My Guide lit a fire, and we sat down to a very sparse supper. There was desultory talk for a time about the wonders of the Heavens spread out above us. We were in the shadow of the mountains and strong purple patches of darkness were sweeping across the Valley of Lhasa as the Sun sank down beyond the Western range. At last all was dark except for the faint twinkling butter lamps from a myriad of houses and lamaseries, and except for the glory of the Heavens above which sent forth their faint twinkling speckles of light.

At last my Guide said, "Now we must go to sleep, Lobsang, there are no temple services tonight to disturb you, no temple services in the morning for which you have to awaken. Sleep well for on the morrow we shall see things that you have never before dreamed possible." So saying, he rolled himself up in his blanket, turned on his side—and went to sleep—just like that. I lay for a time trying to scoop a hole in the rock because my hip bone seemed to stick out a long way, and then I turned on my face for my scars were still causing pain, and then I too eventually went to sleep.

The morning dawned bright. From our altitude in the mountains it was fascinating to watch how the early morning rays of the Sun seemed to shoot horizontally across the valley and illuminate the peaks on the Western horizon with what appeared to be golden fingers of fire. Indeed for a time it looked as if the whole mountain range was afire. We stood and watched, and then simultaneously we turned and smiled at each other.

After a light breakfast—the breakfast always seemed too light for me!—we watered the horses at a small mountain stream, and then, providing them with ample forage which, of course, we had brought with us, we tied them together with about thirty feet space between them. They had plenty of room in which to roam and graze off the sparse grass.

The Lama Mingyar Dondup led the way up the trackless mountainside. By an immense boulder which seemed set immovably into the cliff face, he turned and said, "In your travels you are going to see much which appears to be magic, Lobsang. Here is a first sample of it." Then he turned, and to my horrified amazement he wasn't there any longer! He just disappeared in front of my eyes. Then his voice came from "somewhere" bidding me to step forward. As I did so I found that what appeared to be a strip of moss hanging on the cliff face was, in fact, some loose liands. I approached, and the lama held the fronds aside for me so that I might enter. He turned and I followed him, gazing about me in awe. This seemed to be a wide, wide tunnel, and light was coming in from some source which I could not discern. I followed his receding footsteps, chiding myself for my tardiness, for, as I well realised, if I was going to be too slow I might get lost in this mountain tunnel.

For a time we walked on, sometimes in pitch darkness where I had to feel with a hand lightly brushing the wall at one side. I was not bothered about pits or low hanging rocks because my Guide was very much larger than I and if he had room, well then, there would be room for me.

After some thirty minutes of walking, sometimes in a stifling dead air atmosphere, and sometimes in a bracing mountain breeze, we came to what appeared to be a lighted area. My Guide stopped. I stopped, too, when I reached him and looked about me. I caught my breath in astonishment. This seemed to be a large chamber, I suppose fifty or sixty feet across, and on the walls there were strange carvings, carvings which I failed to understand. It seemed to be very strange people dressed in remarkable clothing which appeared to cover them from head to foot, or, more accurately, from neck to foot because on their heads they had a representation of what seemed to be a transparent globe. Above us, as I looked up, there seemed to be an immense cube, and at the end of that I could just discern a fleecy cloud floating by.

My Guide broke into my thoughts: "This is a very strange area, Lobsang," he told me, "thousands and thousands of years ago there was a mighty civilisation upon this Earth. It was known as the time of Atlantis. Some of the people of the Western world to which in later years you will go think of Atlantis as a legend, as an imaginary place dreamed up by some great story-teller. Well," he mused, "to my regret I have to tell you that many people will think that you have dreamed up your own true experiences, but never mind how much you are doubted, never mind how much you are disbelieved, you know the truth, you will live the truth. And here in this chamber you have proof that there was Atlantis."

He turned and led the way yet further into this strange tunnel. For a time we walked in absolute inky darkness, our breath coming hard in the stale, dead air. Then again there came the freshness, from somewhere a pleasant breeze was blowing. The deadness vanished and soon we saw a glimmer of light ahead of us. I could see my Guide's figure bulking in the tunnel, limmed by light ahead of me. Now with fresh air in my lungs I hurried to catch up with him. Again he stopped in a large chamber.

Here there were more strange things. Someone had apparently carved great shelves in the rock, and on those shelves there were strange artefacts which were without any meaning whatever to me. I looked at them, and gently touched some of these things. They seemed to me machines. There were great discs with strange grooves on them. Some of the discs appeared to be of stone and they were, perhaps, six feet across with an undulating wave on their surface and in the centre of the disc a hole. It meant nothing to me. So I turned from fruitless speculation and examined the paintings and the carvings which adorned the walls. They were strange pictures, large cats who walked on two legs, tree houses with curled cats inside, there were things which seemed to be floating in the air and below on what was obviously the ground humans were pointing upwards at these things. It was all so much above me that it made my head ache.

My Guide said, "These are passages which reach to the ends of the Earth. The Earth has a spine, just as we have Lobsang, but the spine of the Earth is of rock. In our spine we have a tunnel, it is filled with liquid in our case, and our spinal cord goes through. Here this is the spine of the Earth, and this tunnel was man-made in the days of Atlantis when they knew how to make rock flow like water without generating heat. Look at this rock," he said, turning and rapping on a wall. "This rock is fused to almost total hardness. If you take a great stone and slam it against this rock face you would do no harm whatever except to the stone which may shatter. I have travelled extensively and I know that this rocky spine extends from the North Pole to the South Pole."

He motioned that we should sit, so we sat cross-legged upon the floor right beneath the hole which extended up to the open air and through which we could see the darkness of the sky.

"Lobsang," said my Guide, "there are many things on this Earth which people do not understand, there are things inside this Earth too because, contrary to common belief, the Earth is indeed hollow and there is another race of people living inside this Earth. They are more developed than we are, and sometimes some of them come out of the Earth in special vehicles." He stopped and pointed to one of the strange things in the pictures, and then he continued, "These vehicles come out of the Earth and they fly around on the outside of the Earth to see what people are doing and to ascertain if their own safety is jeopardised by the folly of those whom they term "the outsiders."

Inside the Earth, I thought, what a strange place to be living, it must be frightfully dark down there, I don't like the thought of living in the dark, a butter lamp is such a comfort. My Guide laughed at me as he picked up my thoughts, and he said, "Oh, its not dark inside the Earth, Lobsang. They have a Sun something like we have but theirs is much smaller and very much more powerful. They have much more than we have, they are very much more intelligent. But in the days before you, you shall know more about the people of the Inner Earth. Come!"

He rose to his feet and went off through a tunnel which I had not seen, a tunnel diverging to the right, it sloped down, down. We seemed to walk endlessly in darkness. Then my Guide bade me stop where I was. I could hear him fiddling and fumbling about, and there was a clatter that sounded like a rock being moved. Then there were a few sparks as he struck the flint upon steel. There came a dull glow as the tinder ignited, he blew upon it, and then as the tinder burst into small flame he thrust the end of some sort of stick into the flame where it burst into brilliant light.

He held his torch at arm's length slightly above him, and called me to come to his side. I did so and he pointed to the wall in front of us. The tunnel ended and in front of us was an absolutely smooth impenetrable surface which gleamed brightly in the flickering light of the flare. "That, Lobsang," said my Guide, "is as hard as diamond, in fact some of us came here years ago with a diamond and we tried to scratch the surface and we ruined the diamond. This is a passage which leads to the world inside. It was sealed, we believe, by the inside-worlders to save their civilisation during a great flood which struck this Earth. We believe that if this was opened—that is, if we could open it—people would come pouring out and overwhelm us for daring to intrude upon their privacy. We of the higher lama class have often visited this place and tried to commune with those below by telepathy. They have received our messages but they want nothing to do with us, they tell us that we are warlike, that we are as ignorant children trying to blow up the world, trying to ruin peace, they tell us by telepathy that they are keeping check on us and if necessary they will intervene. So we can go no further here, this is the end, this is the blocked line between the upper and the inner worlds. All right, we will go back to the chamber."

He carefully extinguished the flare, and we felt our way back to where the glowing light from the sky above shone down through the hole in the roof.

In that chamber again the lama pointed in another direction, and said, "If we had the strength and the time we could walk right away to the South Pole by following that tunnel. Some of us have covered miles and miles, bringing ample food with us and camping by night, or what we deemed to be night. We travelled endless miles over six months, and at times we came up through a tunnel and found that we were in a strange land indeed but we dared not show ourselves. Always the exits were very very carefully camouflaged."

We sat down and ate our small meal. We had been travelling a long time and exhaustion was setting in for me although my Guide seemed to be immune from exhaustion or even ordinary tiredness. He talked to me and told me all manner of things. He said, "When I was being trained as you are being trained now I too went through the Ceremony of the Small Death, and I was shown the Akashic Record, I was shown the things that had been, and I saw that our Tibet was once a pleasant watering place beside a glittering sea. The temperatures were warm, perhaps even excessively so, and there was profuse foliage and palm trees and all manner of strange fruits which then meant nothing at all to me. But from the Akashic Record I saw a truly wondrous civilisation, I saw strange craft in the sky, I saw people with remarkable cone-shaped heads who walked about, who had their entertainments, who made love, but also made war. Then, as I saw in this Record, the whole country shook and the sky turned black, the clouds were as dark as night, their undersides lit with flickering flames. The land shuddered and opened. It seemed that everything was fire. Then the sea rushed in to the newly opened land, and there were tremendous explosions, explosion after explosion, it seemed that the Sun stood still and the Moon rose no more. People were becoming overwhelmed by tremendous floods of water, people were being seared to death by flames which appeared from I know not where, but the flames flickered with a vile purplish glow, and as they touched people the flesh fell from their bones leaving the skeletons to fall to the ground with a clatter.

"Day succeeded day and the turmoil increased, although one would have said that such a thing was impossible, and then there came a ripping, searing explosion, and everything turned dark, everything was as black as the soot which comes from too many butter lamps burning untrimmed.

"After a time which I could not calculate," he said, "the gloom became lighter, the darkness was diminishing, and when the light of day finally appeared after I know not how long I looked at the picture with utter terror. Now I found that I was looking at a vastly different landscape, the sea was no more, a ring of mountains had sprung up in the darkness and encircled what previously had been the city of a most high civilisation. I looked about me in fascinated horror, the sea had gone, the sea—well, there was no more sea, instead there were mountains and ring upon ring of mountains. Now I could tell that we were thousands of feet higher, and although I was seeing the Akashic Record I was sensing as well, I could sense the rarity of the air, there was no sign of life here, no sign whatever. And as I looked the picture vanished and I found myself back from whence I had started, in the deepest levels of the mountain of Potala where I had been undergoing the Ceremony of the Little Death and given much information."

For a time we sat there meditating upon the past, and my Guide said to me, "I see you are meditating, or attempting to meditate. Now there are two very good ways of meditating, Lobsang. You must be content, you must be tranquil. You cannot meditate with a disturbed mind, and you cannot meditate with a whole gathering of people. You have to be alone or with just one person whom you love."

He regarded me, and then said, "You must always look at something black or at something which is white. If you look at the ground you may be distracted by a grain of pebble, or you may be doubly distracted by some insect. To meditate successfully you must always gaze at that which offers no attraction to the eye, either entire black or pure white. Your eyes then become sick of the whole affair and become, as it were, disassociated from the brain, so then the brain having nothing to distract it optically is free to obey what your sub-conscious requires, and thus if you have instructed your sub-conscious that you are going to meditate—meditate you will. You will find in that sort of meditation that your senses are heightened, your perceptions more acute, and that is the only meditation worthy of the name. In the years which will come to you, you will encounter many cults proffering meditation at a price, but that is not meditation as we understand it nor is it meditation as we want it. It is just something which cultists play with, and it has no virtue."

So saying he rose to his feet exclaiming, "We must get back for the day is far advanced. We shall have to spend another night in the mountains for it is too late to start off for Chakpori."

He set off down the tunnel and I jumped to my feet and scurried after him. I had no desire to be left in this place where inside-worlders, or whatever they liked to call themselves, could perhaps pop up and take me down with them. I did not know what they would be like, I did not know how they would like me, and I certainly did not want to stay alone in the dark of that place. So I hurried,

79

and at last we reached again that entrance by which we had entered.

The horse and the pony were resting peacefully, and we sat down beside them and made our simple preparations for our meal. The light was already far gone, much of the Valley was in darkness. At our altitude the Westering Sun was yet shining upon us, but the orb itself was dipping ever more deeply beneath the mountains on its path to illumine other parts of the world before returning to us.

After some small talk we rolled ourselves in our blankets again and committed ourselves to sleep.

CHAPTER FIVE

Life at Chakpori was hectic. The amount of things I had to learn really shocked me; herbs—where they grew, when to gather them, and be sure that if they were gathered at the wrong time they would be quite useless. That, I was taught, was one of the great secrets of herbalism. The plants, or the leaves, or the barks, or the roots could only be gathered efficiently within the span of two or three days. The Moon had to be right, the stars had to be right, and then the time had to be right also. One must also feel tranquil when gathering such herbs because, so I was told, one who gathered herbs when in a bad mood would make the herbs not worth the taking.

Then we had to dry the things. That was quite a task. Only certain parts of herbs were useful. Some needed to have just the tips of the leaves removed, others needed to have stalks or bark, and each plant or herb had to be treated in its own individual way and regarded with respect.

We took the barks and rubbed them between hands specially cleaned for the purpose—an ordeal in itself!— and so the bark would be reduced to a certain size, sort of granular powder. And then everything had to be laid out on a spotlessly clean floor, no polish on this floor, just rub, rub, rub until there was no dust, no stain, no mark. Then everything was left out and left to Nature to "dry-seal" the virtues of the herb within that which we had before us.

We made herbal tea, that is, infusions of steeped herbs, and I could never understand how people could get the noxious stuff down their throats. It seemed to be an axiom that the worse the taste and the stronger the smell the more beneficial the medicine, and I will say from my own observation that if a medicine is sufficiently evil-tasting the poor wretched patient will get better out of fright rather than take the medicine. It is like when one goes to the dentist, the pain will have vanished so that one hesitates on the doorstep wondering whether one should go through with it. It reminds me rather of the pallid and anxious young man—a recent bridegroom—who was accompanying his very, very pregnant bride to the hospital for "her time was upon her." As he turned before the Reception Desk he said, "Oh gee, honey, are you sure you really want to go through with this?"

As a special student, one who had to learn more, faster, I was not confined only to Chakpori. My time was also devoted to studies at the Potala. Here I had all the most learned lamas, each to teach me his own speciality. I learned various forms of medicine. I learned acupuncture, and in later years, with the weight of many years of experience, I came to the inescapable conclusion that acupuncture was a wondrous thing indeed for those of the East, those who have been long-conditioned to acupuncture. But when, as I found in China, you get sceptical Westerners to deal with—well, unfortunately, they were hypnotised by their own disbelief of anything that didn't come from "God's own country."

There were sacred passages to be seen deep, deep below the mountain of Potala. Down below there was an immense cave with what seemed to be an inland sea. That, I was told, was a remnant of the time so long ago when Tibet was a pleasant land beside the sea. Certainly in that immense cave I saw strange remnants, skeletons of fantastic creatures which much, much later in my life I recognised to be mastodons, dinosaurs, and other exotic fauna.

Then in many places one would find great slabs of natural crystal, and in the natural crystal one could see kelp, different types of seaweed, and occasionally a perfectly preserved fish completely embedded in clear crystal. These were indeed regarded as sacred objects, as messages from the past.

Kite flying was an art at which I excelled. Once a year we went into the high mountains to gather rare herbs and to generally have recreation from the quite arduous life of a lamasery. Some of us—the more foolhardy of us—flew in man-lifting kites, and I thought first that here was that which had been described in the prophecy, but then I came to my senses and realised it could not be a man-lifting kite because these kites were connected to the Earth by ropes, and should a rope be broken or escape from the clutches of the many monks then the kite would fall and there would be the death of the person riding it.

There were quite a number of interviews with the Inmost One, our Thirteenth Dalai Lama, and I felt such love and respect for him. He knew that in a few more years Tibet would be an enslaved state, but "the Gods had foretold" and the Gods must be obeyed. There could be no real form of resistance because there were no real weapons in Tibet. You cannot oppose a man with a rifle when all you have is a Prayer Wheel or a string of beads.

I received my instructions, my sacred orders, from the Great Thirteenth. I received guidance and advice, and the love and understanding which my own parents had completely denied me, and I decided that come what may I would do my best.

There had been times when I had seen my Father. Each time he had turned away from me frozen-faced as if I was the lowest of the low, beneath his contempt. Once, almost at the end of my stay in the Potala, I had visited my parents at home. Mother sickened me by her excess formality, by the manner in which she treated me purely as a visiting lama. Father, true to his belief, would not receive me and shut himself in his study. Yasodhara, my sister, looked at me as if I was some freak or figment from a particularly bad nightmare.

Eventually I was summoned again to the Inmost One's apartments and told much that I do not propose to repeat here. One thing he did tell me was that on the very next week I would go to China to study as a medical student at the University of Chungking. But, I was instructed, I must take a different name, I could not use my own name of Rampa or certain elements of a Chinese rebellion would seize me and use me as a bargaining tool. There was in existence in China at that time a faction devoted to the overthrow of the government and who were prepared to adopt any methods whatever to achieve their objective. So—I was told to pick a name.

Now, how could a poor Tibetan boy, one just approaching manhood, admittedly, but how could he pick a Chinese name when he didn't know anything about China?

I pondered on that awful question, and then unbidden, unexpectedly, a name appeared in my mind. I would call myself KuonSuo which in one dialect of China meant priest of the hill. Surely that was an appropriate name. But it was a name which people found difficult to pronounce— Western people, that is—and so it soon became shortened to Ku'an.

Well, the name was settled. My papers were in order. I was given special papers from the Potala testifying to my status and to the standards I had reached because, as I was told and as I found to be absolutely correct later, Western people would not believe anything unless it was "on paper," or could be felt or torn to pieces. So my papers were prepared and handed to me with great ceremony.

Soon came the day when I had to ride all the way to Chungking. My Guide, the Lama Mingyar Dondup, and I had a most sad farewell. He knew I would not see him again while he was in the body. He gave me many assurances that I would meet him often in the astral.

I had a party of people going with me to protect me from Chinese brigands and to be able to report my safe arrival at Chungking. We started off and rode steadily all along through the Highlands of the Plain of Lhasa, and then we descended to the Lowlands, a place which was almost tropical in the exotic flora—wonderful rhododendrons. We passed many lamaseries, and quite frequently we spent the night in them if they happened to be on our path at a suitable time. I was a lama, actually I was an abbot, and a Recognised Incarnation, thus when we went to a lamasery we were indeed given special treatment. But I did not welcome such special treatment because each time it reminded me of the hardships of my life yet to be endured.

Eventually we left the borders of Tibet, and entered China. Here, in China, every large village seemed to be infested with Russian Communists—white men who were standing up usually on an ox cart telling the workers of the wonders of Communism and how they should rise and massacre those who were land-owners, telling them how China belonged to the people. Well, now apparently it does, and what a mess they have made of it!

The days passed, and our seemingly endless journey became shorter. It was quite annoying to be accosted by certain of the Chinese peasants who gaped at me because I looked somewhat like a Westerner. I had grey eyes instead of brown, and my hair was very dark but still not shiny black, so the story went about that I was a Russian in disguise! Nowadays, since my life in the West, I have had all manner of strange tales told about me; one tale which amused me immensely was to the effect that I was really a German who had been sent to Lhasa by Hitler so that I could learn all the secrets of the occult and then I would come back to Berlin and win the war for Hitler by magical means. Well, in those days I didn't even know there was such a man as Hitler. It is a most remarkable thing how a Westerner will believe everything except that which is utterly true; the more true a matter the more difficult the Westerner finds it to believe. But while on the subject of Hitler and Tibetans, it is a fact that a small group of Tibetans were captured by the Nazis during the war and were compelled to go to Berlin, but they certainly did nothing to help him win the war, as history proves.

At last we turned a corner in the road, and then we came in sight of the old city of Chungking. This city was built on high cliffs and far down below the river flowed. One of the rivers was particularly familiar to me, and that was the Chialing. So the high city of Chungking with its stepped streets with many a cobble was washed at its base by two rivers, the Yangtse and the Chialing. Where the two met a fresh branch was formed, and so the city appeared from afar to be an island.

Seven hundred and eighty steps we climbed up to the city itself. We gazed like yokels at the shops and what to us seemed to be brilliantly lit stores containing articles which were completely beyond our understanding. Things in windows glittered, from many stores came noises, foreigners speaking to each other out of boxes, and then there came blasts of music out of other boxes. It was all a complete marvel to us, and I, knowing that I would have to spend a long time in such surroundings, began almost to quake with fear at the thought.

My retinue were embarrassing me by the manner in which they gaped. Each of the men was shaking with nervousness, and each of them had his mouth open and eyes wide open too. I thought we must look a sorry bunch of country bumpkins gazing like this. But then I thought we weren't here for that, after all. I had to register at the University and so we made our way there. My companions waited in the grounds outside while I entered and made my formal appearance, producing the envelope which I had so carefully safeguarded all the way from Lhasa.

I worked hard in the University. My form of education had been quite different from that which was demanded by the University system and so I had to work at least twice as hard. The Principal of the University had warned me that conditions would be difficult. He said that he had been qualified in the latest American systems and with his very capable staff he was bringing a mixture of Chinese and American medicine and surgery to the students.

The academic work was hard because I knew nothing of Electricity, but I soon learned! Anatomy was easy; I had studied that quite thoroughly with the Disposers of the Dead in Lhasa, and it amused me greatly when first we were ushered into the dissecting rooms where dead bodies lay about to find so many of the students turn a pale green and become violently sick, while others just fainted away on the floor. It was such a simple matter to realise that these dead bodies would not feel anything by our amateurish efforts upon them, they were just like a suit of old clothes which had been discarded and which would be cut up perhaps to make other garments. No, the academic matter was difficult at first, but eventually I was able to take my place quite near the top of the class.

At about this time I noticed that there was a very very old Buddhist priest who was giving lectures at the University, and I made some inquiries and was told, "Oh, you don't want to bother about him, he's just an old crackpot, he's weird!" Well, that persuaded me that I would have to do extra work and attend the "old crackpot's" lectures. It was well worthwhile.

I formally requested permission to attend and was gladly accepted. A few lectures later we were all sitting down and our lecturer entered. As was the custom we rose and remained standing until he told us to be seated. Then he said, "There is no death." No death, I thought, oh, there is going to be a lecture on the occult, he is going to call death "transition" which, after all, is what it is. But the old lecturer let us stew in our own impatience for a time, and then he chuckled and went on, "I mean that literally. If we only knew how we could prolong life indefinitely. Let us look at the process of ageing, and then I hope you will see what I mean."

He said, "A child is born and follows a certain pattern of growth. At a varying age, it varies according to each person, real development is stated to have stopped, real worthwhile growth has stopped, and from then on there is

86

what is known as the degeneration of old age where we get a tall man becoming shorter as his bones shrink." He looked about to see if we were following, and when he saw my particular interest he nodded and smiled most amiably. He continued:—

"A person has to be rebuilt cell by cell so that if we get a cut, part of the brain has to remember the pattern of the flesh before the cut, and then must supply identical, or near-identical, cells to repair the defect. Now, every time we move we cause cells to wear out, and all those cells have to be rebuilt, replaced. Without an exact memory we should not be able to rebuild the body as it was."

He looked about again, then pursed his lips, and said, "If the body, or rather, if the brain forgets the precise pattern then the cells may grow wild, they grow according to no previous pattern and thus those wild cells are called cancer cells. It means that they are cells which have escaped from the control of that part of the brain which should regulate their precise pattern. Thus it is, you get a person with great growths on his body. That is caused by cells growing in haphazard fashion and which have escaped from the brain's control."

He stopped to take a sip of water, and then continued, "Like most of us the growth and replacing centre of the brain has a faulty memory. After reproducing cells for a few thousand times it forgets the precise pattern and with each succeeding growth of cells there is a difference so eventually we have that which we call ageing. Now, if we could remind the brain constantly of the exact shape and size of each cell to be replaced then the body would always appear to be of the same age, always appear to be the same condition. In short, we would have immortality, immortality except in the case of total destruction of the body or damage to the cells."

I thought of this, and then it came to me in a flash that my Guide, the Lama Mingyar Dondup, had told me the same thing in somewhat different words and I had been too young, or too stupid, or both, to understand what he really meant.

87

Our lectures were interesting. We studied so many sub-jects not studied in the West. In addition to ordinary Western type of medicine and surgery we studied acupunc-ture and herbal remedies, but it wasn't all work and no play, although nearly so.

One day when I was out with a friend we wandered down to the shore of the rivers and there we saw an aero-plane which had been parked and just left for some rea-son. The engine was ticking over and the propeller was just revolving. I thought of the kites I had flown, and I said to my friend, "I bet I could fly that thing." He roared with derision, and so I said, "All right, 'I'll show you." I looked around to see there was no one about and I got in that contraption and, to my own surprise and to the sur-prise of many watchers, I did fly the thing but not in the manner prescribed, my aerobatics were quite involuntary and I survived and landed safely only because I had keener reflexes than most.

I was so fascinated with that highly dangerous flight that I learned to fly—officially. And because I showed more than average promise as an airman I was offered a commission in the Chinese forces. By Western standards the style and rank granted to me was Surgeon-Captain.

After I had graduated as a pilot the commanding officer told me to continue my studies until I had graduated also as a physician and surgeon. That was soon done, and at last, armed with quite a lot of official looking papers, I was ready to leave Chungking. But there came a very sad message concerning my Patron, the Thirteenth Dalai Lama, the Inmost One, and so, obeying a summons, I returned to Lhasa for a very brief time.

Destiny called, however, and I had to follow the dic-tates of those in authority above me and so I retraced my steps on to Chungking and then on to Shanghai. For a time I was on the reserve as an officer of the Chinese forces. The Chinese were having a most difficult time be-cause the Japanese were trying to find an excuse to invade China. All manner of indignities were being heaped upon foreigners in the hope that the foreigners would make trouble for the government of China. Men and women were being stripped naked in public and given a body search by Japanese soldiers who said they were suspecting the foreigners of taking messages. I saw one young woman who resisted; she was stripped naked and made to stand for hours in the centre of a busy street. She was truly hysterical, but every time she tried to run away one of the sentries would prod her obscenely with a bayonet.

The Chinese people watching could do nothing, they did not want an international incident. But then one old Chinese woman threw a coat to the young woman so that she could cover herself; a sentry jumped at her and with one slash cut off the arm that had thrown the coat.

It amazes me now, after all I have seen after all I have suffered, that people the world over seem to be rushing to the Japanese offering them friendship, etcetera, presumably because they offer in return cheap labour. The Japanese are a blight upon the Earth because of their insane lust to dominate.

In Shanghai I had my own private practise as a doctor, and a quite successful one too. Perhaps if the Japanese war had not started I should have made my living in Shanghai, but on the 7th July, 1937, there was an incident at the Marco Polo Bridge, that incident really started the war. I was called up and sent to Shanghai docks to supervise the assembling of a very large three-engine aeroplane which had been stored there ready for collection by a firm which had proposed to start a passenger airline.

With a friend I went to the docks and we found the aeroplane in pieces, the fuselage and the wings all separate. The undercarriage was not even connected, and the three engines were separately crated. By dint of much psychometry and even more attempts at the use of commonsense I managed to direct workers to assemble the aircraft on a very large open space. As far as I could I checked everything over, I examined the engines, made sure they had the right fuel and the right oil. One by one I started those engines and tried them out, let them idle and let them roar, and when I was satisfied after many adjustments that they would keep going I taxied that three-engined plane up and down that large tract of land so that I would get used to the feel of the thing because one doesn't stunt too long in a three-engined plane!

At last I was satisfied that I understood the controls and could handle them quite well. Then with a friend who had a tremendous amount of faith in me, we got into the plane and taxied to the extreme edge of the wide open space. I had coolies put large chocks in front of the wheels with instructions to pull on the ropes to move the chocks immediately I raised my right hand. Then I opened all three throttles so the plane roared and shook. At last I raised my hand, the chocks were pulled out, and we cavorted madly across the ground. At the last moment I pulled back on the control and we went up at what I believe was a truly unorthodox angle, but we were flying, and we flew around for an hour or two to get the feel of the thing. Eventually we came back to the landing space and I was careful to note the direction of smoke. I came in slowly and landed into the wind, and I confess that I was bathed in perspiration; my friend was, too, in spite of all his faith in me!

Later I was told to remove the plane to another area where it could be guarded day and night because the international brigade was becoming very active, and some of these foreigners thought they could do just what they liked with the property of the Chinese. We did not want our big aeroplane damaged.

At a secluded base the plane was altered. Much of the seating was removed and stretchers were put in on racks. At one end of the plane there was a metal table fitted and this was going to be an operating theatre. We were going to do emergency operations because now—at the end of 1938—the enemy were approaching the outskirts of Shanghai, and I had instructions to close my practise which I had still been carrying on part-time. I was told to take the plane to a safe area while it could be repainted, all white and with a red cross. It also was to have "Ambulance Plane" painted on it in Chinese and Japanese characters.

But when painted the paint was not destined to last very long. Bombs were dropping over Shanghai, the air was full of the acrid stench of explosives, full of particles of grit which stung the nostrils, irritated the eyes—and scoured the paint from Old Abie, as we called our aeroplane. Soon there came a greater "crump" and Abie jumped into the air and collapsed flat on the underside of the fuselage, a near bomb burst had blown off the undercarriage. With immense labour and considerable ingenuity we repaired the undercarriage with lengths of split bamboo, like putting splints on a broken limb, I thought. But with the bamboo lashed firmly in place I taxied up and down the bomb-pitted ground to see how the ship would manage; it certainly seemed to be all right.

We were sitting in the plane when there was a great commotion and an irate Chinese general—full of pomp and self-assurance—came on to our airfield surrounded by subservient members of his staff. Brusquely he ordered us to fly him to a certain destination. He would not take our statement that the plane really was not fit to fly until further repairs had been carried out. He would not accept our statement that we were an ambulance plane and were not permitted by international law to carry armed men. We argued, but his argument was stronger; he just had to say, "Take these men and shoot them for failing to obey military orders," and that would have been the end of us. We would have gone flying off without him!

The troop of men climbed into the plane tossing out medical equipment—just scattering it out of the open door —to make room for their own comforts. Out went our stretchers, out went our operating table, our instruments, everything. They were just tossed away as if they were garbage and would never be wanted again. As it happened they weren't.

We took off and headed toward our destination, but when some two hours away from our point of departure Red Devils came out of the Sun, Japanese fighter planes, hordes of them like a load of mosquitoes. The hated red symbol glowed brightly from the wings. They circled our ambulance plane with the red crosses so prominently displayed, and then quite callously they took turns to pump bullets in us. Since that time I have never liked the Japanese, but I was to have more fuel for the flame of my dislike in days to come.

We were shot down and I was the only one left alive. I fell into about the most unsalubrious place in China—a sewage ditch where all the waste matter was collected. And so I fell into the sewage ditch and went all the way to the bottom, and in that incident I broke both ankles.

Japanese soldiers arrived and I was dragged off to their headquarters and very, very badly treated indeed because I refused to give them any information except that I was an officer of the Chinese services. It seemed to annoy them considerably because they kicked out my teeth, pulled off all my nails, and did other unpleasant things from which I still suffer. For instance, I had hoses inserted in my body and into the water supply was put mustard and pepper, then the taps were turned on and my body swelled enormously and tremendous damage was caused inside. That is one of the reasons I suffer so much even now, all these years later.

But there is no point in going into detail because an interested person can read it all in "Doctor from Lhasa." I wish more people would read that book to let them see what (well, YOU know what!) sort of people the Japanese are.

But I was sent to a prisoner-of-war camp for women because this was considered to be degrading. Some of the women had been captured from places like Hong Kong. Some of them were in truly shocking condition because of continual rapes.

It is worth mentioning that at this time there were certain German officers who were "advising" the Japanese, and these officers were always provided with the best looking of the women, and the perversions—well, I have never seen anything like it. It does seem that the Germans excel not merely at making war but at "other things" as well.

After a time, when my ankles had healed and my nails

had regrown, I managed to make an escape, and I made my slow painful way back to Chungking. This was not yet in the hands of the Japanese and my medical colleagues there did wonders in restoring my health. My nose had been broken. Before being broken it had been —according to Western standards—somewhat squat, but now through the exigencies of surgery my nose became quite a large affair which would have done credit to any Westerner.

But war came to Chungking, the violent war of Japanese occupation. Once again I was captured and tortured, and eventually I was again put in charge of a prison camp where I did the best I could for patients among the prisoners. Unfortunately a senior officer was transferred from another area, and he recognised me as an escaped prisoner.

All the trouble started again. I had both legs broken in two places to teach me not to escape. Then they put me on a rack and pulled my arms and legs very tight indeed. In addition, I had such a blow across the lower spinal region that grave complications were caused which even now are making my spine degenerate, so much so that I can no longer stand upright.

Once again, after my wounds healed, I managed to escape. Being in an area where I was well-known I made my way to the home of certain missionaries who were full of "tut tut's" and great exclamations of sorrow, compassion —the works. They treated my wounds, gave me a narcotic—and sent for the Japanese prison guards because, as they said, they wanted to protect their own mission and I was not "one of them."

Back in the prison camp I was so badly treated that it was feared that I should not survive, and they wanted me to survive because they were sure I had information they needed, information which I refused to give.

At last it was decided that I escaped far too easily, and so I was sent to the mainland of Japan to a village near the sea, near a city called Hiroshima. I was again put in charge—as medical officer—of a prison camp for women, women who had been brought from Hong Kong, Shanghai, and other cities, and who were being kept there with some dim view on the part of the Japanese that they could be used as hostages when bargaining later because the war was going very badly for the Japanese now, and the leaders knew full well that they had no hope of winning.

One day there was the sound of aircraft engines, and then the ground shook and an immense pillar appeared in the distance, a pillar the shape of a mushroom with rolling clouds spreading high into the sky. About us there was utter panic, the guards scattered like scared rats, and I, ever alert for such an opportunity, vaulted over a fence and made my way down to the waters edge. A fishing boat was there—empty. I managed to climb aboard and with a pole just had enough strength left to push the boat into deeper water. Then I collapsed into the stinking bilge. The boat swept out to sea on the tide which was receding, but I—up to my neck in water in the bottom of the boat— knew nothing about it until at last I dizzily awakened and it came back to me with a start that once again I had escaped.

Painfully I dragged myself up a bit higher out of the water and looked anxiously about. The Japanese, I thought, would be sending out speedboats to capture a many-time runaway. But no, there were no boats at all in sight, but on the skyline over the city of Hiroshima there was a dull, evil, red glow and the sky was black, and from that blackness there dropped "things," blood-red splotches, sooty masses, black greasy rain.

I was aching with hunger. I looked about and found a locker in the side of the bulkhead toward the bows, and in that locker there were pieces of stale fish which presumably were meant to be used as bait. They were sufficient to maintain a certain amount of life in me, and I was most grateful to the fisherman who had left them there.

I lay back across the seats of the boat and felt great unease because the boat was rocking in a most strange manner, the sea itself seemed strange, there were waves of a type I had not seen before almost as if there was an underwater earthquake.

I looked about me and the impression was eerie. There

94

was no sign of life. Normally on such a day there would have been innumerable fishing boats about because fish was the staple food of the Japanese. I felt a great sense of unease because being telepathic and clairvoyant I was obtaining remarkable impressions, so confused and so many that I just could not understand them.

All the world seemed to be quiet except for a strange sighing of the wind. Then high above me I saw a plane, a very large plane. It was circling about and through being observant I could see the large lens of an aerial camera pointing down. Obviously photographs were being taken of the area for some reason which I then did not know.

Soon the plane turned about and went off beyond the range of my vision, and I was alone again. There were no birds in sight; strange, I thought, because sea birds always came to fishing boats. But there were no other boats about either, there was no sign of life anywhere, and I had these peculiar impressions coming to my extra-senses. At last I suppose I fainted because everything suddenly went black.

The boat with my unconscious form drifted on into the Unknown.

CHAPTER SIX

After what seemed endless days, and actually I had no idea how long it was, but after this indeterminate period I suddenly heard harsh foreign voices and I was lifted by arms and legs and swung in an arc and let go. I landed with a splash just at the edge of the water and opened bleary eyes to find that I had reached some unknown shore.

Before me I saw two men pushing frantically on the boat, and then at the last moment jumping aboard. Then sleep, or coma, claimed me again.

My sensations were rather peculiar because I suddenly

had the impression of swaying, and then a cessation of motion. After—I was told later—five days I returned to the Land of the Living and found myself in a spotlessly clean hovel which was the home of a Buddhist priest. I had been expected, he told me haltingly, for our languages were similar yet not the same and we found difficulty in making ourselves understood.

The priest was an old man and he had had dreams (he called them dreams, anyway) that he had to stay and render assistance to a "great one who would come from afar." He was near death through starvation and age. His brownish-yellow face looked almost transparent he was so under-nourished, but from somewhere food was obtained and over several days my strength was built up. At last, when I was thinking that I must be making my way on through life's path, I awakened in the morning to find the old monk sitting beside me cross-legged—and dead. He was stone cold, so he must have died in the early part of the night.

I called in some of the people from the small hamlet in which the hovel was and we dug a grave for him, and gave him a decent burial complete with Buddhist ceremonial.

With that task done I took what scant supply of food was left and set out on my way.

Walking was awful. I must have been far weaker than I had imagined because I found myself left sick and dizzy. But there was no turning back. I did not know what was happening, I did not know who was an enemy or who was a friend, not that I had had many friends in my life. So I pressed on.

After what seemed to be endless miles I came to a frontier crossing. Armed men were lounging about near a frontier station, and I recognised their uniforms from pictures I had seen; they were Russians, so now I could place my location, I was on the road to Vladivostok, one of the great Russian sea-ports of the far East.

At the sight of me the frontier guards set great mastiffs loose and they came snarling and slavering at me, but then, to the amazement of the guards, they jumped at me with affection because they and I recognised each other as friends. Those dogs had never been talked to telepathically before and I suppose they thought I was one of them. Anyway, they jumped all around me and welcomed me with wild yelps and barks of joy. The guards were most impressed, they thought I must have been one of them and they took me into their guard room where they gave me food. I told them that I had escaped from the Japanese, so, as they were at war with the Japanese as well, I automatically became "on their side."

Next day I was offered a ride to Vladivostok so that I could look after the dogs who were being taken back to the city because they were too fierce for the guards. Gladly I accepted the offer and the dogs and I rode in the back of a truck. After a rather bumpy ride we arrived at Vladivostok.

Again I was on my own, but as I was turning away from the guard room in Vladivostok a tremendous noise of screams, howls, and snarling barks rent the air. Some of the dogs in the large compound had suddenly been afflicted with blood-lust and were attacking guards who were trying to control them. A Captain came and after hearing what his frontier men had told him he ordered me to control the dogs. By good fortune I managed to do just that, and by telepathy I got the dogs to understand that I was their friend and they would have to behave themselves.

I was kept in that camp for a month while the dogs were being retrained, and when the month was over I was permitted to go on my way again.

My task now was to satisfy that terrible urge I had of moving on, moving on. For a few days I hung about Vladivostok wondering how to reach the main city, Moscow. At last I learned about the Trans-Siberian railway, but one of the dangers here was that many escapees wanted to get to Moscow and for quite a distance by the sidings there were pits in which guards lay in wait so they could see beneath the trains and shoot off anyone clinging to the rods.

At last one of the men from the Vladivostok border patrol with whom I had been for the last month showed me how to circumvent the guards, and so it was that I went to Voroshilov where there were no checks on the railway. I took food with me in a shoulder bag and lay in wait for a suitable train. Eventually I managed to get aboard and I lay beneath, between the wheels, actually I tied myself to the bottomside of the railroad car floor so that I was quite high up above the axles and hidden by the grease boxes. The train started and for about six miles I endured being held by ropes until I decided it was safe to climb aboard one of the railroad cars. It was dark, very dark, the Moon had not risen. With extreme effort I managed to slide open one of the railroad car doors and painfully climb inside.

Some four weeks after, the train came to Noginsk, a small place about forty miles from Moscow. Here, I thought, was the best place to get off, so I waited until the train slowed for a bend and then I dropped safely to the frozen ground.

I walked on and on, and it was a disturbing sight indeed to see corpses beside the road, the corpses of people who had died from starvation. An elderly man, tottering in front of me, dropped to the ground. Instinctively I was about to stoop and see what I could do for him when a whispered voice came, "Stop Comrade, if you bend over him the police will think you are a looter and will shoot you. Keep on!"

In time I reached the centre of Moscow, and was gazing up at the Lenin Monument when suddenly I was felled to the ground by, I found, a blow from a rifle butt. Soviet guards were standing over me just kicking me and repeatedly kicking me to get me to rise to my feet. They questioned me, but they had such a "big city" accent that I was completely unable to follow what they were talking about, and at last, with two men guarding me, one at each side, and a third man with a huge revolver poking into my spine, I was marched off. We reached a dismal building, and I was just shoved into a small room. Here I was interrogated with considerable roughness, and I gathered that there was a spy scare in Moscow and I was considered to be some sort of a spy trying to get into the Kremlin!

After some hours of being kept standing in a small closet the size of a broom cupboard, a car arrived and I was taken off to the Lubianka Prison. This is the worst prison in Russia, it is the prison of tortures, the prison of death, a prison where they have their own built-in crematorium so that all the evidence of a mutilated body could be burned.

At the entrance to Lubianka, or in a small vestibule, I had to remove my shoes and go barefooted. The guards with me put thick woollen socks over their boots and then I was marched in dead silence along a dim corridor, a corridor that seemed miles long. There was no sound.

A strange hiss sounded, and the guards pushed me in the back with my face against the wall. Something was put over my head so that no light could be seen. I sensed rather than felt someone passing me, and after some minutes the cloth over my head was roughly jerked away and I was pushed forward once more.

After what seemed to be an impossible time a door was opened in utter silence, and I was given a very violent push in the back. I stumbled forward and fell. There were three steps but in the pitch darkness of the cell I could not see them; so I fell and knocked myself unconscious.

Time passed with incredible slowness. At intervals there came screams ululating on the quivering air, and dying off with a gurgle.

Some time later guards came to my cell. They gestured for me to go with them. I went to speak and was smashed across the cheeks, while another guard put a finger to his lips in the universal sign of "No talk!" I was led out along those endless corridors again, and eventually found myself in a brilliantly lit interrogation room. Here relays of questioners asked me the same questions time after time, and when I did not vary my story two guards were given special instructions; I was given an abbreviated tour of the

Lubianka. I was taken along the corridors and I was shown torture rooms with poor unfortunate wretches undergoing the tortures of the damned, both men and women. I saw such tortures, such bestial performances, that I would not dare repeat them because, knowing Western people, I know that I would be disbelieved.

I was shown into a stone room which had what appeared to be stalls. From a blank wall stone stalls extended about three feet from the wall, and the guards showed me how a man or woman was pushed naked into a stall with hands upon the wall in front. Then the prisoner would be shot through the back of the neck and would fall forward, and all the blood would run into a drain and so no unnecessary mess was caused.

The prisoners were naked because, according to Russian thought, there was no point in wasting clothing, clothing which could be used by the living.

From that place I was hurried out along another corridor and into a place which looked like a bake-house. I soon saw that it was not a bake-house because bodies and pieces of bodies were being cremated. As I arrived a very burned skeleton was being removed from a furnace and was then dumped into a great grinder which revolved and ground up the skeleton with a horrid crunching noise. The bone dust, I understood, was sent to farmers as fertilizer, as was the ashes.

But there was no point in keeping on about all the tortures that I underwent, but it will suffice to say that at long last I was dragged before three high officials. They had papers in their hands which, they said, testified to the fact that I had helped influential people in Vladivostok and another that I had helped his daughter escape from a Japanese prisoner-of-war camp. I was not to be killed they told me but would be sent to Stryj, a city in Poland. Troops were going there from Russia and I would go with them as a prisoner and then in Stryj I would be deported from Poland also.

Eventually after a lot more delay because I was really too ill to be moved and so had to be given time to recover

—eventually I was handed over to a Corporal who had two soldiers with him. I was marched through the streets of Moscow to the railway station. The weather was freezing cold, bitterly cold, but no food was offered although the three soldiers wandered off one at a time to get food.

A big detachment of Russian soldiers came into the station, and a sergeant came across saying that the orders had been changed and I was going to Lwow instead. I was loaded aboard the train which went off with many a shudder and jolt, and at long last we arrived at the city of Kiev.

Here I and some of the soldiers entered a troop carrier, to be accurate, forty soldiers and I were crammed into one. And then the troop carrier raced off, but our driver was too fast and too inexperienced, he caromed into a wall and the troop carrier exploded in fire from the broken fuel tank. For quite a time I was unconscious. When I did recover consciousness again I was being carried into a hospital. Here I was X-rayed, and it was found that I had three broken ribs, one broken end had perforated my left lung. My left arm was broken in two places, and my left leg was broken again at the knee and at the ankle. The broken end of a soldier's bayonet had penetrated my left shoulder, only just missing a vital place.

I awakened from an operation to find a fat woman doctor smacking my face to bring me back to consciousness. I saw that I was in a ward with forty or fifty other men. The pain I had was incredible, there was nothing to ease the pain, and for quite a time I hovered between life and death.

On the twenty-second day of my stay in the hospital two policemen came to the ward, ripped the blanket off my bed, and bawled at me: "Hurry up, you're being deported, you should have left three weeks ago!"

I was taken to Lwow and told that I would have to pay for my hospital treatment by working for a year repairing and rebuilding the roads of Poland. For a month I did that, sitting beside the road breaking stones, and then because my wounds were not properly healed I collapsed

101

coughing blood, etcetera, and was taken off to a hospital again. Here the doctor told me that I would have to be moved out of the hospital as I was dying and he would get into trouble if any more prisoners died that month because he had "exceeded his quota."

So it was that I was deported and, once again, became a wanderer. For the first of many times I was told that I had only a little while to live, but like many times since, I did not die.

Walking along a road I saw a car in distress, with a very frightened man standing beside it. Well, I knew quite a lot about cars and aircraft engines, so I stopped and found there was nothing much wrong with the car, nothing I couldn't put right, anyhow. So I managed to get it going and he was so extremely grateful that he offered me a job. Now, that is not so strange as it may seem because that car had passed me some time ago, we had been crossing a river bridge together, crossing just where the border guards were stationed. He had been stopped a long time, and I suppose he had been watching the pedestrians and wondering what they were doing, where they were going—anything to pass away idle moments. I got over the border in very quick time—about the only time in my life that I have! But, he offered me a job and I could see by his aura that he was a reasonably honest man, as honest as he could afford to be, in other words. He told me that he needed to have cars taken to different locations, so I took his offer and it afforded me a truly wonderful opportunity of seeing Europe.

He knew the location quite well and he had "contacts." He looked at my papers and shuddered at the sight of them, telling me that I couldn't possibly get anywhere except prison if I had papers marked "Deportee." So he left me by the roadside for a time, after which he came back for me and drove me to a place—I will not say where—where I was fitted out with fresh papers, a forged passport, and all the necessary travel documents.

So I drove for him. He seemed to be scared of driving and it was fortunate for me that he was. I drove to Bratislava and on to Vienna; Vienna, I could see, had been a very wonderful city indeed but now it was knocked about a lot because of the aftermath of war. We stayed there two or three days, and I looked around the city as much as I could although it wasn't easy because the people were inordinately suspicious of foreigners. Every so often a person would sidle up to a policeman and there would be whispered conversation, and then the policeman would make sure his gun was in order and then he would approach me and demand, "Papers!" It gave me a good chance to check that my papers were quite "authentic" because there was never any query at all about them.

From Vienna we went to Klagenfurt. There was only a slight delay there, I waited about eight hours and got thoroughly frozen in the drizzling rain which came teeming down. I also got quite hungry because there was rationing and I hadn't got the right sort of coupons. But hunger was a thing to which I was well accustomed, so I just put up with it.

We drove through the night to Italy and made our way to Venice. Here, to my regret, I had to stay ten days, unhappy ten days they were, too, because I am gifted or cursed with an absolutely exceptional sense of smell and, as possibly everyone knows, the canals of Venice are open sewers. After all, how can you have closed-in sewers when the whole darn place is flooded? So it certainly was not a place to swim!

The ten days dragged, the place seemed to be full of Americans who were very full of money and drink. It was an everyday sight for Americans to flash an immense roll of money which would have kept most of the Italians for a year. Many of the Americans, I was told, were deserters from the U.S. army or air force who had quite big businesses in black market goods.

From Venice we went on to Padua, a place rich in history and redolent of the past. I spent a week here, my employer seemed to have a great amount of business to do and I was dazzled by the different girl friends he picked up as other people pick flowers by the roadside. No doubt it was because he had such a big bank roll.

In Padua my employer had a sudden change of plans, but he came to me one day and told me all about it, saying he had to fly back to Czechoslovakia. But—there was an American, he said, who very much wanted to meet me, a man who knew all about me, so I was introduced to this man. He was a great beefy man with thick blubber lips, and a girl friend who did not seem to mind whether she was draped or undraped. The American was another man dealing in cars, trucks, and various other types of machinery. I drove a big truck for a time in Padua, my load was different official cars, some taken from high-ranking Nazis and others from Fascist officials who had lost life and cars. These cars—well, I just could not understand what was happening to them, but they seemed to be exported to the U.S.A. where they fetched fabulous prices.

My new employer, the American, wanted me to take a special car to Switzerland, and then take another car to Germany, but, as I explained, my papers were not good enough for that. He pooh-poohed my arguments, but then said, "Gee, I got the very thing for you, I know what we can do. Two days ago a drunken American drove into a concrete abutment and he was splattered all over the place. My men got his papers before they were even touched by the blood which came out of him; here they are." He turned and rifled through his big bulging briefcase and fished out a bundle of papers. I jumped to instant alertness when I saw that they were the papers of a ships Second-Engineer. Everything was there, the passport, the Marine Union card, work permits, money—everything. Only one thing was wrong; the photograph.

The American laughed as if he would never stop and said, "Photograph? Come on with me, we'll get that done right away!" He bustled me out of the hotel room and we went to some peculiar place which meandered down many stone steps. There were secret knocks on the door and a sort of password, and then we were admitted to a sleazy room with a gang of men lounging around there. I could see at a glance that they were counterfeiters although I couldn't tell what sort of money they were forging, but that was nothing to do with me. The problem was explained to them, and my photograph was speedily taken, my signature was taken as well, and then we were ushered out of the place.

The following evening there came a knock on the hotel door and a man entered carrying my papers. I looked through them and I really could believe that I had signed the things and filled in all the details with my own handwriting, they were so perfect. I thought to myself, "Well, now I've got all the papers I should be able to get aboard a ship somewhere, get a job as an Engineer and go off to the U.S.A. That's where I have to be, the U.S.A., so I'll do what this fellow wants in the hope I'll get to some big seaport."

My new employer was delighted with my change of attitude so the first thing he did was to give me a large sum of money and introduce me to a Mercedes car, a very powerful car indeed, and I drove that car to Switzerland. I managed to get through Customs and Immigration, and there was no trouble at all. Then I changed the car at a special address and continued on to Germany, actually to Karlsruhe, where I was told that I had to go on to Ludwigshafen. I drove there, and to my surprise found my American employer there. He was delighted to see me because he had had a report from his contacts in Switzerland that the Mercedes had been delivered without a scratch on it.

I stayed in Germany for some three months, a little more than three months as a matter of fact. I drove different cars to different destinations, and frankly it simply did not make sense to me, I didn't know why I was driving these cars. But I had plenty of time to spare so I made good use of it by getting a lot of books to study marine engines and the duties of a ships Engineer. I went to Maritime Museums and saw ship models and models of ships' engines, so at the end of three months I felt quite confident that I could turn my engineering knowledge to marine engineering also.

One day my boss drove me out to a deserted airport. We drew up in front of a disused aircraft hangar. Men rushed to open the doors, and inside there was a truly weird contraption which seemed to be all yellow metal struts, the thing had eight wheels and at one end was a truly immense scoop. Perched at the other end was a little glassed-in house, the driving compartment. My employer said, "Can you take this thing to Verdun?" "I don't see why not," I replied. "Its got an engine and its got wheels, so it should be driveable." One of the mechanics there showed me how to start it and how to use it, and I practised driving up and down the disused aeroplane runways. An officious policeman rushed into the grounds and announced that the thing could only be used at night and it would have to have a man at the rear end to watch out for coming traffic. So I practised while a second man was found. Then, when I was satisfied that I knew how to make the machine move and, even more important, knew how to make the thing stop, my look-out and I set off for Verdun. We could only drive by night because of German and French road regulations, and we could not exceed twenty miles an hour so it was a slow journey indeed. I had time to watch the scenery. I saw the gutted countryside, the burned-out wrecks of tanks and aircraft and guns, I saw the ruined houses, some with only one wall still remaining. "War," I thought, "what a strange thing it is that humans treat humans so. If people only obeyed our laws there would be no wars. Our law: Do unto others as you would have them do unto you, a law which would effectively prevent wars."

But I saw some very pleasant scenery too, but I was not getting paid to admire the scenery, I was getting paid to get that clattering hunk of machinery safely to Verdun.

At last we arrived at that city, and early in the morning before there was much traffic I drove it into an immense construction yard where we were expected. Here a very grim looking Frenchman who seemed to be more or less

106

square rushed out at me, and said, "Now take this thing to Metz!" I replied, "No, I have been paid to bring it here and I am driving it no further." To my horrified amazement he whipped out one of those awful knives which have a spring—you press a button and the blade slides out and locks in place. He came at me with that knife, but I had been well trained, I wasn't going to be stabbed by a Frenchman, so I did a little karate throw which sent him down on his back with one awful clatter, his knife spinning from his hand. For one awful moment he lay there dazed, then with a bellow of rage he jumped to his feet so fast that his feet were moving before they touched the ground, and he dashed into a workshop and came out with a three foot bar of steel used for opening crates. He rushed at me and tried to bring the bar down across my shoulders. I dropped to my knees and grabbed one of his legs, and twisted. I twisted a bit harder than I intended because his leg broke with quite a snap at the knee.

Well, I expected to get arrested by the police at least. Instead, I was roundly cheered by the man's employees, and then a police car drove up with the police looking very grim indeed. When they were told what had happened they joined in the applause, and to my profound astonishment they took me off for a good meal!

After the meal they found accommodation for me, and when I was in that accommodation a man came along and told me that he had heard all about me and did I want another job. Of course I did, so he took me out to a cafe in which there were too elderly ladies obviously waiting for me. They were very very old and very very autocratic, they did a bit of the "my man" talk until I told them that I wasn't their man, I didn't want anything to do with them in fact. And then one of them laughed outright and said she really did admire a man with spirit.

They wanted me to drive them in a very new car to Paris. Well, I was all for that, I wanted to go to Paris, so I agreed to drive them to Paris even though there was the stipulation that I must not exceed thirty-five miles an hour. That was no problem to me, I had just driven from Ludwigshafen at twenty miles an hour!

I got the two old ladies safely to Paris and they paid me very well for the trip, and gave me many compliments on my driving, actually they offered to take me in their service because they said they liked a man with spirit to be their chauffeur, but that was not at all what I wanted. My task had not yet been accomplished, and I did not think much of driving old ladies about at thirty-five miles an hour. So I refused their offer and left them to try to find another job.

People with whom I left the old ladies' car suggested accommodation for me, and I made my way there arriving just as an ambulance arrived. I stood outside waiting for the commotion to end and I asked a man what it was all about. He told me that a man who had an important job taking furniture to Caen had just fallen and broken his leg, and he was worried because he would lose his job if he could not go or find a substitute. As he was carried out on a stretcher I pressed forward and told him that I could do his job for him. The ambulance men halted a moment while we talked. I told him I wanted to go to that city, and if he could fix it he could get paid for the trip and I would go just to get that transport. He looked overjoyed in spite of the pain in his leg, and said that he would send a message to me from his hospital, and with that he was loaded into the ambulance and driven away.

I booked in at the lodging house, and later that night a friend of the furniture remover came and told me that the job was mine if I would go to Caen and help unload furniture and load a fresh lot. The man, he told me, had accepted my offer that he would have the money and I would have the work!

At the very next day, though, I had to be off again. We had to go to one of the big houses in Paris and load up this great pantechnicon. We did so—the gardener of the estate and I—because the driver was too lazy. He made excuse after excuse to leave. At last the pantechnicon was loaded and we departed. After we had done about a mile, or less, the driver stopped and said, "Here, you take on driving, I want to get some sleep." We shifted positions, and I drove on through the night. In the morning we were at Caen and drove to the estate where the furniture and luggage had to be unloaded. Again one of the house staff and I unloaded because the driver said he had to go elsewhere on business.

In the late afternoon when all the work was done the driver appeared and said, "Now we must go on and load a fresh lot." I got into the driving seat and drove on as far as the main railroad station. There I jumped out, taking all my possessions with me, and said to the driver, "I've been working all the time, now you do some for a change!" With that I went into the station and got a ticket for Cherbourg.

Arrived at that city I wandered about a bit and eventually took a room at the Seamen's Lodgings in the dock area. I made quite a point of meeting as many ships Engineers as I could and making myself agreeable to them, so with a little prodding on my part I received opportunities to see their engine rooms aboard their ships, and I received many many hints and pointers which could not easily be obtained from text books.

Day after day I went to shipping agents showing "my" papers and trying to get a berth as second engineer on a ship going to the U.S.A. I told them that I had come to Europe on vacation and had been robbed of my money and now I had to work my way back. There were many expressions of sympathy, and at last a good old Scottish Engineer told me that he would offer me a job as third Engineer going that night to New York.

I went aboard the ship with him, and down the iron ladders to the engine room. There he asked me many questions about the operation of the engines and about the keeping of records and watches. Eventually he expressed himself as entirely satisfied and said, "Come on up to the Master's quarters, and you can sign the ship's articles." We did that and the ship's Master looked a grim sort of fellow; I didn't like him at all, and he didn't like me either, but we signed the articles and then the ship's First Engineer told me: "Get your dunnage aboard, you take first duty, we sail tonight." And that was that. And so, very probably for the first time in history a lama of Tibet, and a medical lama at that, posing as an American citizen, took a job aboard an American ship as Third Engineer.

For eight hours I stood engine room watch. The Second was off duty, and the First Engineer had work to do connected with leaving port, so I had to go immediately on duty without any opportunity to have a meal or even to change into uniform. But eight hours duty in port was a blessing to me. It enabled me to get accustomed to the place, to investigate the controls, and so instead of being displeased and unhappy about it as the Chief expected me to be, really I was well content.

After the eight hours was up the Chief Engineer clattered down the steel ladder and formally relieved me of duty, telling me to go and have a good meal because, he said, I looked famished. "And be sure," he commanded, "to tell the cook to bring down cocoa for me."

It was not a happy ship by any means. The Captain and the First Officer thought they were commanding a first-class liner instead of a beat-up old tramp steamer, they insisted on uniform, they insisted on inspecting one's cabin, an unusual thing aboard ship. No, it was not a happy ship indeed, but we thudded along across the Atlantic, rolling and swaying in the North Atlantic weather. At last we reached the light-ship at the approach to New York harbour.

It was early morning and the towers of Manhatten seemed to be agleam with reflected light. I had never seen anything like this before. Approaching from the sea the towers stood up like something out of one's fevered imagination. We steamed on down the Hudson and under a great bridge. There I saw the world-famed Statue of Liberty, but to my astonishment Liberty had her back to New York, had her back to the U.S.A. This shocked me. Surely, I thought, unless America was going to take all and sundry then the liberty should be in the U.S.A.

We reached our berth after much shoving and towing by small tugs with a big "M" on the funnel. Then there was the roaring of motors, great trucks arrived, the cranes started to work as a shore crew came aboard. The Chief Engineer came and begged me to sign on, offering me promotion to Second Engineer. But no, I told him, I had had enough of that ship, some of the deck officers had indeed been an unpleasant lot.

We went to the shipping office and signed off, and the Chief Engineer give me a wonderful reference saying that I had shown great devotion to duty, that I was efficient in all branches of engine room work, and he made a special note that he invited me to sign on again with him at any time in any ship because, he wrote, I was a "great shipmate."

Feeling quite warmed by such a farewell from the Chief Engineer and carrying my heavy cases I went out of the docks. The din of traffic was terrible, there were shouting people and shouting policemen, and the whole place seemed to be absolutely mad. First I went to a ships hostel, or, more accurately it should be described as a seamen's hostel. Here again there was no sign of hospitality, no sign of friendship, in fact with quite average politeness, I thought, I thanked the person for handing me the key to a room. He snarled back at me, "Don't thank me, I'm just doing my job, nothing more."

Twenty-four hours was the limit that one could stay in that hostel, forty-eight if one was going to join another ship. So the next day I picked up my cases again, went down in the elevator, paid off the surly reception clerk, and walked out into the streets.

I walked along the street being very circumspect because I was, frankly, quite terrified of the traffic. But then there was a terrific uproar, cars sounding their horns, and a policeman blowing his whistle, and at that moment a great shape mounted the sidewalk, hit me and knocked me down. I felt the breaking of bones. A car driven by a driver under the influence of drink had come down a one-way street, and as a last attempt to avoid hitting a delivery truck had mounted the sidewalk and knocked me over.

I awakened much later to find myself in a hospital. I had a broken left arm, four ribs broken, and both feet smashed. The police came and tried to find out as much as they could about the driver of the car—as if I had been his bosom friend! I asked them about my two cases and they said quite cheerily, "Oh no, as soon as you were knocked down, before the police could get to you, a guy slithered out of a doorway, grabbed your cases and went off at a run. We didn't have time to look after him, we'd got to get you off the sidewalk because you were obstructing the way."

Life in the hospital was complicated. Because of the rib injuries I contracted double-pneumonia and for nine weeks I lingered in that hospital making a very slow recovery indeed. The air of New York was not at all like that to which I was accustomed, and everyone kept all the windows closed and the heat turned on. I really thought I was going to die of suffocation.

At last I made enough recovery to get out of bed. After nine weeks in bed I was feeling dreadfully weak. Then some hospital official came along and wanted to know about payment! She said, "We found $260 in your wallet and we shall have to take two hundred and fifty of that for your stay here. We have to leave you ten dollars by law, but you'll have to pay the rest." She presented me with a bill for over a thousand dollars.

I was quite shocked and complained to another man who had come in after her, a man who appeared to be some senior official. He shrugged his shoulders and said, "Oh well, you'll have to sue the man who knocked you down. Its nothing to do with us." To me that was the epitome of foolishness because how could I trace the man when I hadn't seen him? As I said, I had more money in my cases, and the only reply was, "Well, catch the man and get your cases back from him." Catch the man—after nine weeks in hospital, and after the police apparently had failed to make any worthwhile attempt to catch him. I was quite shocked, but I was to be shocked even more. The man—the senior official—produced a paper and said, "You are being released from hospital now because you have no money for any further treatment. We can't afford to keep you foreigners here unless you can pay. Sign here!"

I looked at him in shock. Here was I, the first day out of bed for nine weeks, I had had broken bones and double-pneumonia, and now I was being turned out of hospital. There was no sympathy, no understanding, and instead I was literally—and I mean this quite literally—turned out of hospital, and all I had was a suit of clothes I was wearing and a ten dollar bill.

A man in the street to whom I explained my problem jerked a thumb in the direction of an employment agency, and so I went there and climbed up many stairs. At last I got a job with a very very famous hotel indeed, a hotel so famous that almost anyone in the world will have heard of it. The job—washing dishes. The pay—twenty dollars a week and one meal a day, and that one meal a day was not the good stuff that guests had, but the bad stuff left by guests or which was not considered fit for the guests. On twenty dollars a week I could not afford a room, so I did not bother about such things, I made my home wherever I happened to be, trying to sleep in a doorway, trying to sleep beneath a bridge or under an arch, with every so often the prod of a policeman's night stick in my ribs, and a snarling voice bidding me to get out of it and keep moving.

At last, by a stroke of luck, I obtained a job with a radio station. I became a radio announcer, talking to the whole world on the short waves. For six months I did that, and during that six months I obtained from Shanghai papers and belongings which I had left with friends there. The papers included a passport issued by the British authorities at the British Concession.

But, as I began to feel, I was wasting my time as a radio announcer, I had a task to do, and all I was earning now was a hundred and ten dollars a week which was a great advance over twenty dollars a week and one meal, but I decided to move on. I gave the radio station adequate time

113

to obtain a suitable replacement for me, and when I had trained him for two weeks I left.

Fortunately I saw an advertisement wanting people to drive cars, so I answered the advertisement and found that I could take a car and drive it all the way to Seattle. There is no point in recounting the journey now, but I drove safely to Seattle and got a bonus for careful driving and for turning in the car without a single scratch on it. And then—I managed to go on to Canada.

So ends the second book
The First Era.

BOOK THREE

The Book of Changes.

"Let not thy sorrows obtrude on to those who have left this World of Man."

"Name no names, for to name those who have passed beyond this realm is to disturb their peace."

"Wherefore it is that those who are mourned suffer greatly from those who mourn."

"Let there be Peace."

· · · · · ·

It also makes Good Sense,
the Law of Libel being what it is!
Wherefore I say unto you—
Names shall not be named.

PAX VOBISCUM.

CHAPTER SEVEN

There is little point in describing how I made my way through Canada, all the way through the Rocky Mountains, and all along to Winnipeg, to Thunder Bay, Montreal, and Quebec City. Thousands of people—tens of thousands of people—have done that. But I did have some unusual experiences which I may yet write about, although that is not for this moment.

In my journey through Canada it was borne upon me that I should make my way to England. I was convinced that the task which I still had to do had to start in England, a little place which I had seen only from afar from the porthole of a ship leaving Cherbourg and heading out into the English Channel before turning for the U.S.A.

In Quebec I made inquiries and managed to obtain all necessary papers such as passport, work permit, and all the rest. I also managed to obtain a Seaman's Union card. Again, there is no point in going into details of how I obtained these things. I have in the past told bureaucrats that their stupid system of red tape only strangles people who have all papers legitimately; in my own case I state emphatically that the only time I have had any difficulty at all entering a country was when my papers were in order. Here in Canada, when I used to be more mobile and could go to the U.S.A., there was always difficulty with my papers; there was always something wrong, something for the Immigration officer to quibble about. So, bureaucrats are parasites who should be eliminated like lice. Hey! That would be a good idea, too, wouldn't it?

I made my way back to Montreal and there, with my papers perfectly in order I was able to get aboard a ship as a deckhand. The pay was not wonderful, but my own idea

117

was that I wanted to get to England, and I had no money for a ticket, therefore any pay was better than having to pay.

The work was not too hard, it consisted merely of re-arranging cargo and then knocking wedges into hold covers. Soon we were steaming up the English Channel, and not too long after we turned into the Solent on our way to Southampton. I was off duty at the time and was able to sit in the stern and look out across the English scenery which attracted me considerably, the English scenery seemed to me to be of the greenest of greens—at that time I had not seen Ireland which can beat the English scenery any time—and so I was quite entranced.

The Military Hospital at Netley intrigued me vastly. I thought from the water that it must be the home of a king or someone of such status, but a member of the crew with quite a loud laugh soon told me that this was just a hospital.

We went up past Woolston on the right, and Southampton on the left. I was interested to see at Woolston the home of the supermarine flying boats which were making very much of a name for themselves in the Far East.

Soon we docked in Southampton, and officials came aboard, checked the ship's papers and examined the crews' quarters. Finally we were given clearance to go ashore and I was on the point of leaving but was called back for Immigration check once again. The officer looked at my papers and was very friendly and approving when in answer to his question, "How long are you staying?" I replied, "I am going to live here, sir." He put the necessary stamps on the passport and gave me directions for seamen's lodgings.

I walked out of the Immigration office and stood for a moment taking a last look at the old freighter on which I had arrived from the New World to the Old. A Customs officer started to move across with a smile on his face, and then suddenly there was a stunning blow at my back and I reeled against a wall, dropping my two cases as I did so.

Gathering my scattered wits I turned around and saw a man sitting at my feet. He was a senior Customs officer who had been hurrying to work and had misjudged his distance trying to get in the door. I went to help him up and he struck my outstretched hands with a fury of hatred. I recoiled in complete astonishment, the accident was not my fault, I was just standing there inoffensively. But I picked up my cases to move on when he yelled at me to stop. He called two guards to detain me. The Customs officer I had seen in the office hurried out and said, "Its quite all right, sir, quite all right. His papers are perfectly in order." The senior official seemed to go black in the face with fury, and no one could get a word in. On his orders I was taken to a room where my cases were opened and everything thrown on to the floor. He found nothing wrong here. So he demanded my passport and other papers. I gave them to him and he leafed through them and then snarled that I had a visa and a work permit and I didn't need both. With that he tore my passport across and threw it in the garbage bin.

Suddenly he stooped, picked up all the papers and crammed them in his pocket so that, I suppose, he could destroy them elsewhere.

He rang a bell and two men came from the outer office. "This man has no papers," said the senior officer, "he will have to be deported. . . ." "But," said the officer who had stamped my papers, "I saw them, I stamped them myself." The senior turned to him enraged and said such things that made the poor man turn pale. And so eventually I was taken to a cell and left there.

The next day a simpering young idiot from the Foreign Office came, stroked his baby face and agreed with me that I must have had the necessary papers. But, he said, the Foreign Office could not have trouble with the Immigration Office so I would have to be sacrificed. The best thing I could do, he said, would be to agree that my papers had been lost overboard, otherwise I should be lodged in prison for quite a time and after the end of my sentence I should still be deported. Two years in prison was a thought that did not suit me at all. So I had to sign a paper saying that my passport had been lost at sea.

"Now," said the young man, "you will be deported to New York." This was too much for me because I had left from Montreal and Quebec, but the answer was quick; I had to go to New York because if I went to the Province of Quebec and told my story the press might get hold of it and make a commotion, because the press were always avid for anything sensational—not from a point of view of doing anyone any good but just because the press thrived —and thrive—on sensation and on trouble.

I was kept in a cell for a time, and then one day I was told I was to be deported the next day. In the morning I was led out of the cell and the senior officer was there beaming with joy that he, petty little bureaucrat that he was—had managed to subvert justice to his own wishes.

In the afternoon I was taken to the ship, and told that I would have to do work, and it would be the hardest work aboard ship, trimming coal in the bunkers of one of the oldest of old coal burners.

Then I was taken back to the cell because the ship was not yet ready to leave and the Captain could not accept me aboard until an hour before departure time. Twenty-four hours later I was taken to the ship and locked in a very small cabin where I was kept until the ship sailed beyond territorial limits.

After a time I was released from the cell, for that is what the small cabin was, and then given a battered shovel and rake and told to clean out the clinkers, etcetera.

So I sailed back across the Atlantic, back toward New York, and as the first loom of land appeared in the morning the Captain sent for me and spoke to me alone. He told me that he agreed I had been unjustly treated. He told me that the police were coming aboard to arrest me and I would be sentenced for illegal entry into the U.S.A., and then after serving a sentence I would be deported to China. He looked about him, and then went to a drawer in his desk saying, "A man like you can easily escape if you want to. The biggest difficulty is the handcuffs. Here is a key which will fit American handcuffs, I will turn away and you can take the key. As you can understand I cannot give you the key, but if you take it—well, I need know nothing about it."

So saying he turned, and I quickly pocketed the key.

That Captain was a very decent man indeed. As the U.S. police came aboard clinking their handcuffs he told them that I was not likely to cause any trouble, he told them that in his own opinion I had done nothing wrong and I was just being framed by an unpleasant Immigration officer. The senior policeman laughed cynically and said that he quite agreed, every man was being framed by someone else, and with that he snapped the handcuffs on my wrists and gave me a rough punch toward the Jacob's ladder—the ladder by which pilots and policemen enter and leave ships still at sea.

With some difficulty I managed to get down the ladder although the police were expressing hopes that I would fall in and they would have to fish me out. Aboard the police launch I was roughly pushed down in the stern. Then the two policemen went about their job of filling in a report and turning their launch towards the shore.

I waited my chance until the wharves were near, and then when the police were not looking in my direction I just jumped over the side.

The water was dreadful. There was a thin scum of oil and filth on the surface, filth which was the sewage of the ships and liners docked there, filth which had blown off the wharves, floating newspapers, floating boxes, bits of coke, all manner of strange pieces of wood just floating by. I dived deep and managed to get hold of the key and unlock the handcuffs which I let drop to the bottom of the harbour.

I had to come up for air, and as I broke surface there was a fuselage of shots quite close to me, so close that one of the bullets spattered water in my face. So, with a quick gulp of air, I sank down again and struck out not for the closest ward-pilings, but one rather more distant with the thought that the police would expect me to swim for the nearest.

Slowly I let myself rise to the surface until only my mouth and chin were above water. Then again I took a deep breath, and another, and another. No shots came my way, but I could just barely see the police launch cruising about in front of the nearer wharf.

Gently I let myself sink again and swam slowly—to conserve my air supply—to the wharf.

There was a sudden bump, and instinctively my hands went out and clasped on that which I had bumped my head. It was a mess of half-sunken timbers which apparently had fallen from the partly ruined wharf above me. I clung to that with just my face out of the water. Slowly, as I could hear no sound, I sat up and in the distance I could see the police launch which had been joined by two others prowling about beneath the piles of the other wharf. On top of the wharf armed police were dashing around searching various buildings.

I kept still because suddenly a boat came along with three policemen in it. They were rowing silently. One of the policemen had a pair of binoculars and he was scrutinising all the wharves in the area. Slowly I slid off the beam and let myself sink in the water so that only my nose and mouth were above the surface. Eventually I raised my head a bit and the boat was a long way away. As I looked I heard a shout, "Guess the guy's a stiff by now, we'll pick up his body later."

I lay again on the beam shivering uncontrollably in the coldness of wet clothing and the stiff breeze which blew across me.

When darkness was falling I managed to get on to the top of the wharf and darted for the shelter of a shed. A man was approaching and I saw he was a Lascar, and he looked quite friendly so I gave a low whistle. He strolled nonchalantly on and, quite without purpose it seemed, he edged toward my hiding place. Then he stooped to pick up some pieces of paper which were lying about. "Come out cautious like," he said, "a coloured gentleman is waiting with a truck, he'll get you out of this."

Well, eventually I did get out of it, but I was in a sorry state indeed, I was suffering from exhaustion and from exposure. I got into the garbage truck, a tarpaulin was stretched over me, and a whole load of garbage dumped on top!

The coloured man took me to his home and I was well looked after, but for two days and nights I slept the sleep of the totally exhausted.

During my exhaustion, while the physical body was repairing itself, I made an astral journey and saw my beloved Guide and friend, the Lama Mingyar Dondup. He said to me, "Your sufferings have truly been great, too great. Your sufferings have been the sour fruit of man's inhumanity to Man, but your body is getting worn out and soon you will have to undergo the ceremony of transmigration.

In the astral world I sat and my companion sat with me. I was told more.

"Your present body is in a state of collapse, the life of that body will not continue much longer. We feared that such conditions would prevail in the wild Western world that you would be impaired, and so we have been looking about for a body which you could take over and which in time would reproduce all your own features.

"We have determined that there is such a person. His body is on a very very low harmonic of your own, otherwise, of course, a change could not take place. The bodies must be compatible, and this person has a body which is compatible. We have approached him in the astral because we saw that he contemplated suicide. It is a young Englishman who is very very dissatisfied with life, he is not at all happy with life, and for some time he has been trying to decide on the most painless method of what he calls 'self-destruction.' He is perfectly willing to leave his body and journey here to the astral world provided he doesn't lose by it!

"We persuaded him a little time ago to change his name

123

to that which you are now using, so there are a few more things to be settled and then—well, you will have to change bodies."

It was very, very necessary, I was instructed, that I should return to Tibet before I could undergo the necessary process of transmigration. Careful instructions were given to me and when I felt well enough I went to a shipping office and took passage to Bombay. Once again I was subjected to all manner of harassment because my luggage consisted of just one case. But at last I got aboard the ship and when I was in my cabin two detectives came to visit me to find out why I had only one case. Assured that I had adequate luggage in India they smiled happily and went away.

It was most strange being a passenger aboard ship. Everyone avoided me because I was a pariah who had only one case of luggage. The others, of course, seemed to have enough luggage to stock a whole store, but I—apparently the poorest of the poor—must be a fugitive from justice, or something, to travel as I did, and so I was avoided.

The ship went from New York all the way up along the coast of Africa and through the Straits of Gibraltar. Then we made another stop at Alexandria before entering the Suez Canal, and so on to the Red Sea. The Red Sea was terrible, the heat was murderous, and I almost got heat stroke. But finally we passed the coast of Ethiopia, crossed the Arabian sea, and docked at Bombay. The noise and smell in Bombay was terrible, fantastic in fact, but I had a few friends, a Buddhist priest and a few influential people, and so my weeks stay in Bombay was made interesting.

After the week in which I tried to recover from all the shocks and strains I had had I was put on a train and crossed India to the city of Kalimpong. I managed to drop off the train before it actually entered Kalimpong because I had been warned that the place was absolutely thronged with Communist spies and newspaper men, and new arrivals were stopped and questioned by newspaper men and—as I found to be true later—if one would not give an interview the newspaper men "invented" one without any regard whatever to the truth.

I knew Kalimpong slightly, certainly I knew enough to get in touch with some friends and so "went underground," away from spies and away from newspaper men.

By now my health was deteriorating very rapidly, and there were serious fears that I would not live long enough to undergo the ceremony of transmigration. A lama who had been trained at Chakpori with me was in Kalimpong and he came to my assistance with very potent herbs.

I moved on in the company of this medical lama and after ten weeks of hard travel we reached a lamasery overlooking the Valley of Lhasa. It was high and inaccessible, it was inconspicuous, and Communists would not bother about such a small insignificant place. Here again I rested, I rested for some seven days in all. On the morrow, I was told one day, I should journey into the astral and meet the astral body of the man whose physical vehicle I was going to take over.

For the present I rested, and mused upon the problems of transmigration. This person's body was not of much use to me because it was HIS body and had a lot of vibrations incompatible with my own. In time, I was told, the body would conform exactly to my own body when at that same age, and if Westerners find this a difficult matter to believe or understand, let me put it like this; the Western world knows about electro-plating, and the Western world also knows about electro-typing. In the latter system an article can be immersed in a certain fluid and a special "connector" is applied opposite the article, and when current is turned on at the correct rate and amperage an exact duplicate of the original item is built up. This is known as electro-typing.

Again, it is possible to do electro-plating. One can plate in a variety of metals, nickel, chromium, rhodium, copper, silver, gold, platinum, etcetera. One merely has to know how to do it. But the current flows from one pole to another through a liquid, and the molecules of one pole are transferred to the other pole. It is a simple enough system, but this is not a treatise on electro-plating. Transmigration and the replacing molecule by molecule of the "fabric" of the host by that of the—what shall I say?— new occupant is very real, it has been done time after time by those who know how. Fortunately those who know how have always been people of reliable character, otherwise it would be a terrible thing indeed if one did just take over another person's body and do harm. I felt rather smug, foolishly so perhaps, when I thought that—well, I am going to do good, I don't want to take over anyone else's silly body, all I want is peace. But it seemed there was to be no peace in my life.

In passing, and as one who has studied all religions, I must point out that Adepts did it for life after life. The Dalai Lama himself had done so, and the body of Jesus was taken over by the Spirit of the Son of God, and it had been common knowledge even in the Christian belief until it was banned because it made people too complacent.

From my high viewpoint in this remote isolated lamasery I could look out upon the distant city of Lhasa; quite a powerful telescope had somehow been smuggled out of the Potala and brought here, so one of my idle amusements was to use the telescope and look at the surly Chinese guards at the Pargo Kaling. I saw the troops rushing about in their jeeps, I saw through that telescope many unspeakable things done to men and to women, and I recalled with great horror that I had fought on the side of the Chinese as had many others, and now the Chinese were not behaving according to their promises, according to their avowed principles. All they thought of was violence.

It was hard to believe, looking out of the glassless window, that this was the same Tibet, the same Lhasa, that I had known before. Here the golden Sun still struck gleaming rays through ravines in the mountains, the silvery Moon still traversed the blackness of the night sky, and the distant pinpoints of coloured light which were the stars still stabbed down through the roof of Heaven. Night birds

126

did not call, though, as of yore because the Chinese Communists killed everything on sight. To my horror I found that they were extinguishing the life of those creatures I loved so much. Birds, they say, ate the grain which would cause humans to starve. Cats were killed, so no longer, so I was told, were there any cats left in Lhasa. Dogs were killed and eaten by the Chinese. It seemed to be a Chinese delicacy. So not only poor humans were being subjected to death at the hands of the Chinese Communists, animals too, the pets of Gods, were being exterminated for no worthwhile reason. I was sick at heart at all the horrors being perpetrated on a harmless, innocent people. As I gazed out at the darkening sky I was overcome with emotion, overcome with sorrow, and then I thought, well I have this job to do, much evil has been forecast in my life. I hope I am strong enough to endure all that which has been foretold.

For some time I had been dimly aware of much excitement, of an air of expectancy, and my attention had been drawn again and again to Lhasa. The telescope was wonderful. But it was difficult looking out through a slit window with such a cumbersome article, so I turned to a pair of twenty magnification binoculars which also had been brought and which offered greater manoeuvreability for views beyond the angle of the telescope in the window.

My attention was suddenly distracted from looking out for three men entered, two of them supporting the one between them. I turned and looked at him in horror; he was blind, his eyes had been gouged out leaving red pools. His nose was missing. The two men with him gently helped him to a sitting position, and in fascinated horror I recognised him as one that I had known before, as one who had helped me with my studies at Chakpori. The two attendants bowed and left. The lama and I were facing each other, and he spoke in a low voice: "My brother," he said to me, "I can well discern your thoughts. You wonder how I got in a condition like this. I will tell you. I was out about my lawful occasion and I happened to glance up toward Iron Mountain. A Chinese Communist officer sud-

127

denly turned from where he was sitting in his car and accused me of staring at him and thinking evil thoughts towards him. Naturally I denied the charge for such was not the truth, I was merely looking at our beloved home. But no, the officer said that all priests were liars and reactionists, and he gave abrupt orders to his men. I was seized and knocked down, and then a rope was put around my chest and knotted behind my back. The other end was tied to the rear of the car in which the officer sat. Then, with a whoop of joy, he drove off dragging me face down on the road."

The old lama stopped and lifted his robe. I gasped with horror because all the skin and much of the flesh had been torn off from head to foot, shreds of flesh hung down, and the inside of his robe was just a bloody mess. He carefully lowered his robe again, and said, "Yes, the roughness of the road tore off my nose, it tore off other things too, and now I am waiting to pass over to the Land Beyond. But before I can have that release I have one more task to do."

He paused for a moment or two, getting back some energy, and then said, "This matter of transmigration and the possibility that we might have to use it has been known for many years, and I was in charge of the project, I had to study the ancient manuscripts to find out as much as I could about it. I had to consult the Akashic Records and I had to amass as much knowledge as I could." He paused again, but then went on, "The Chinese eventually released me from my bonds but the officer had one more evil deed to do. He kicked me as I lay on my back in the dirt and said, 'You stared at me and you wished me evil, for that you shall stare no more.' One of his men picked up a sharp narrow flint from the roadway and stuck it in my eyeballs, one after the other, and just flipped my eyeballs out so that they dangled on my cheeks. Then with a laugh they went away and left me as I was, with my nose ripped off, my body ripped and torn, no longer would one be able to say if I was a man or a woman because such parts had been torn off, and on my cheeks rested my blinded eyes with the orbs perforated and the fluid spilling out and running down to my ears.

"When they were able to, shocked people came to my aid and I was lifted up and carried into a house. I fainted, and when I recovered consciousness I found that my eyes had been removed and I had been well treated with herbal packs. Stealthily by night I was carried up into the mountains to await your coming. Now I have to tell you much, and to accompany you into a journey into the astral from which I shall not return."

He rested yet awhile that he might regain a little of his strength, and then when a slight colour was returning to his cheeks he said, "We must go into the astral."

So we went the familiar route again. Each of us was sitting in the lotus position, that position which we of the East find the easiest to maintain. We said our suitable mantras with which our vibrations were so heightened that with the almost imperceptible jerk which accompanies such transition we departed from our bodies, I temporarily and my companion permanently.

The greyness of Earth and the white of the eternal snows departed from our sight. Before us there appeared a veil, a veil which shimmered bluish-white, a veil which as one first approached it appeared to be an impenetrable barrier, but those who knew how could enter without hindrance. This we did, and found ourselves in an area of glorious light with impressions of joy.

At that point of the astral world which we entered we were upon a green sward, the grass was short and springy beneath our feet. "Ah!" breathed the lama with me, "How wonderful to see again, how wonderful to be without pain. Soon my task will be finished then I shall be Home for a time at least." So saying he led me along a pleasant path.

There were trees about, many many trees, all in green and red and yellow leaf. To the side of us there swept a majestic river, mirroring in its watery surface the deep blue of the sky above. Faint fleecy clouds drifted lazily across the sky and there was an atmosphere of bubbling life, of vitality, of health, of happiness.

129

In the trees birds sang, birds of a type which I had not seen on Earth for these were glorious creatures indeed, birds of many different colours, birds of many different plumage.

The old man and I walked on among the trees, and then we came to an open space which was indeed a garden, a garden of brilliant flowers, none of a type that could be recognised by me. The flowers seemed to nod toward us as if greeting us. In the distance I could see people wandering about as if they were luxuriating in this glorious garden. Every so often a person would bend and sniff a flower. At times others would reach up skywards, and a bird would come and land on his outstretched hand. There was no fear here, only peace and contentment.

We walked on a while, and then before us we saw what seemed to be an immense temple. It had a cupola of shining gold and the walls which supported it were of a light fawn colour. Other buildings stretched away from it, each in a pastel shade, all in harmony, but at the entrance to the temple a group of people were waiting. Some of them wore the robes of Tibet, and another—I could not understand what he was wearing for the moment, it looked as if he was wearing black or something very dark. And then I saw as we approached that it was a man of the Western world attired in Western raiment.

At our approach the lamas turned and spread their hands in our direction, spread their hands in welcome. I saw that one of them was my Guide and friend, the Lama Mingyar Dondup, so I knew that all would be well for this man was good and good only. Another figure I saw was even more eminent when upon the earthly plane, but now he was just one of the welcoming "committee" awaiting us.

Our happy greetings were soon exchanged, and then as one we moved into the body of the great temple, traversing the central hall and moving further into that building. We entered a small room the existence of which was not easy to discern, it appeared as if the walls slid away and, admitting us to its presence, closed solidly behind us.

My Guide, obviously the spokesman, turned to me and said, "My brother, here is the young man whose body you are going to inhabit." I turned and faced the young man aghast. Certainly there was no resemblance at all between us, he was much smaller than I, and the only resemblance between us was that he was bald the same as I! My Guide laughed at me and shook an admonitory finger at my nose: "Now, now, Lobsang," he laughed, "not so quick with your decisions. All this has been planned, first I am going to show you some pictures from the Akashic Record." And this he did.

Upon completing our viewing of the Record he said, addressing the young man, "Now young man, I think it is time that you told us something about yourself, for if one is to take over your body then it certainly is time for the one taking over to know that with which he is faced."

The young man, so addressed, looked very truculent indeed and replied in sullen tones, "Well, no, I have nothing to say about my past, it has always been held against me. Whatever I do say about my past it will only be used to pull me down." My Guide looked sadly at him and said, "Young man, we here have vast experience of these things and we do not judge a man by what his parentage is alleged to be but what that man is himself." My Guide sighed and then said, "You were going to commit the mortal sin of suicide, a sin indeed, a sin which could have cost you dear in many many lives of hardship to atone. We offer you peace, peace in the astral, so that you may gain understanding of some of those things which have troubled you throughout your life. The more you cooperate the more easily can we help you as well as helping that task which we have before us." The young man shook his head in negation, and said, "No, the agreement was that I wanted to leave my body, you wanted to stuff someone else in it, that's all the agreement was, I hold you to it."

Suddenly there was a flash and the young man disappeared. The old lama with me, who was now a young man in full health, exclaimed, "Oh dear, dear, with such truculent thoughts he could not stay with us here on this astral plane. Now we shall have to go to where he is sleeping in a room alone. But for this night we must let him sleep, we do not want to injure the body, so I shall have to return somehow to Lhasa with you until the next night."

Time passed, and I could see that the old lama was failing rapidly, so I said to him, "Time we went into the astral." "Yes," he replied, "I shall not see this body of mine again. I must go, we must go, for if I die before I am in the astral that will delay us."

Together we encountered that jerk and soared on and upwards, but not into the astral world we had visited before. This time we soared across the world to a house in England. We saw in the physical the face of the man whom I had previously seen only in the astral. He looked so discontented, so unhappy. We tried to attract his attention but he was sleeping very soundly indeed. The old lama whispered, "Are you coming?" I whispered, "Are you coming?" And we kept it up, first one and then the other, until at last very very reluctantly the astral form of this man emerged from his physical body. Slowly it oozed out, slowly it coalesced above him in the exact shape of his body, then it reversed its position, head of the astral body to the feet. The form tilted and landed on his feet. He certainly looked very truculent and, I could see, he had absolutely no recollection of seeing us before. This was astounding to me, but my companion whispered that he had been in such a bad temper and had slammed back in his body so violently that he had completely obliterated all memories of what had happened to him.

"So you want to leave your body?" I asked. "I most certainly do," he almost snarled back at me. "I absolutely hate it here." I looked at him and I shuddered with apprehension and, not to put too fine a point upon it, with pure fright. How was I going to take over the body of a man like this? Such a truculent man, so difficult. But, there it was. He laughed and said, "So YOU want my body? Well, it doesn't matter what you want, it doesn't matter who you are in England, all that matters is who do you know, how much have you got."

We talked to him for a time and he grew calmer and I said, "Well, one thing, you will have to grow a beard. I cannot shave my beard because my jaws have been damaged by the Japanese. Can you grow a beard?" "Yes, sir," he replied, "I can and I will."

I thought for a moment and then I said, "Very well, you should be able to grow a suitable beard in a month. In one month's time, then, I will come and I will take over your body and you shall be allowed to go to an astral world so that you may recover your tranquility and know that there is joy in living." Then I said, "It would help us greatly, greatly, if you would tell us your life story because although we have seen much in the astral by way of the Akashic Records there still is a boon to be derived by hearing the actual experiences from the person concerned."

He looked dreadfully truculent again, and said, "No, no I cannot bear to speak of it, I am not going to say another word."

Sadly we turned away and went into the astral world so that we could again consult the Akashic Record to see much of his life, but in the Akashic Record one sees all that has happened, one does not necessarily get the unspoken opinions of a person, we see the act but not the thought which preceded the act.

But let us now take a leap forward from those days many years ago. The young man now, many many years in the astral world, has mellowed somewhat and to some small extent appreciates the difficulties with which we are confronted. He has, then, agreed to tell us his own life story. He upon the astral world, and I, Lobsang Rampa, here upon the world of Earth trying to write down precisely as dictated those things which the young man tells. We will have his story shortly, but it is necessary to emphasise that names will not be given for they cause distress to others. This is not a story of vengeance, this is not a story of bitterness. Actually, it is a story in this book of triumph over seemingly impossible obstacles. There have been many attempts to stop my books but I have ever been mindful of the way a man steps forth, even though dogs be yapping at his feet; I have ever been mindful that a man can continue his work even though midges and blowflies swarm about him. So I say, I have no need for bitterness for that which I wanted to do is now possible, and my present task is just to complete the task of another who "fell by the roadside."

Again, I say with the utmost sincerity at my command that all these books of mine are true, utterly true, they are written without authors' license, they contain the truth as these things happened to me. All the things that I write about I can do, but not for public exhibition because I am neither charletan nor showman. The things I do are for the completion of my task.

So now let us turn the page and read what there is that the young man said.

CHAPTER EIGHT

This is the story of the life of the Host. It is a story which is difficult in the telling because the teller is on the astral plane and the one who has to transcribe it is upon the earth plane in the city of Calgary, Alberta, Canada. This life story is out of context, it interposes a break between that which has already been written and the part which naturally would continue, but when one is dealing with affairs of the astral then one has to make some concessions in the matter of time because time on the astral plane is not the same as time on the earth plane. Hence this life story is being given now, and the explanation as to why it is being now is made here to avoid a spate of letters asking all manner of questions. From this point on, then, and until I so indicate everything written is dictated by the one whom we will call the "Host."

134

Grandfather was a very important man indeed, at least in the rural district of Plympton which, so far as I remember, included Plympton St. Mary, Plympton St. Maurice, Underwood and Colebrook, together with quite a number of other sub-locations.

Grandfather was Chief of the Waterworks of Plympton. Every day he used to go in pony and trap all the way up the hill until a mile or so uphill he came to an enclosed mound with a little hut on it, the reservoir was covered in. Grandfather used to go up there with a four foot stick, one end of which was saucer shaped and the other rounded. He used to walk about with his ear to the saucer shaped end, the other end he put in contact with the ground and he could hear the water rushing through the pipes below to feed the taps of Plympton, Underwood, Colebrook, and other districts.

Grandfather also had quite a thriving business, employing several men and a lot of apprentices. He taught them plumbing—hence the scurrilous tales which later were to arise—tinsmithing, and general engineering. In those days, right at the start of the century, people did not rush to supermarkets to obtain kettles, saucepans, frying pans, and all the rest of it; these things were made by hand, and Grandfather's men made them.

Grandfather lived at Mayoralty House in Plympton St. Maurice, the house really had been the house of the Mayor and it was right opposite the Guildhall and the Police Station.

Mayoralty House consisted of four to five acres of land divided into three sections. The first section abutted from the four storey house and formed a walled garden of probably just under an acre. In that garden near the house there was a grotto built of very large pebbles and with windows of various coloured glasses. Outside that there was a small lawn with flowers and plants all along the edges. In the middle there was a large fish pond nicely tiled and with a fountain and with waterwheels at the two ends. A jet of water could be turned on and the waterwheels would spin around. Then there was a little bob which went down into the water, and at certain times of the day fish would pull on that bob and a bell would ring and then they would be fed.

Facing the fish pond there were two large wall aviaries, very carefully maintained and thoroughly cleaned. In these there were two dead trees fixed against the wall and it provided an ideal spot for the very tame birds. The birds were so tame that when Grandfather went into the aviaries, by opening the doors of course, none of the birds flew out.

Further down to that first part of the garden there was a greenhouse, one of Grandfather's joys. And beyond that a small orchard.

Outside that walled garden there was a private roadway which left the main street and went down under part of Mayoralty House—which went as a bridge across that roadway and at the bottom there were what had been malthouses in days gone by. The malthouses were not used when I knew them because it was much cheaper, apparently, to ship malt in to Plympton from a few hundred miles away.

By the malthouse there was the Fire Station. Grandfather owned the Fire Brigade and he had horses which drew the fire engines to the scene of the fire. He did all this as a public service, but if businesses or big households were saved from burning down then Grandfather, of course, charged them a reasonable fee. But for poor people he made no charge. The fire engines were very well maintained and they were manned by volunteers or by his own staff.

Here, too, there were the yards where much of his outdoor equipment was kept, wagons and things like that. Here, too, he had two peacocks which were his pride and joy and which always came to him when he made certain noises.

One went through that yard and through a gate into a garden which was, I suppose, about two and a half or three acres in extent. Here he grew vegetables, fruit trees, and the whole garden was extremely well cared for.

Beneath the house—beneath that four storey house—there were workshops without any windows but seemingly well ventilated. Here master craftsmen, tinsmiths, coppersmiths, and apprentices worked, and they had to work quite hard too.

Grandfather had two sons as well as a daughter. Both sons were thrust willy-nilly into apprenticeship. They had to learn general engineering, tinsmithing, coppersmithing —and the ubiquitous plumbing, and they had to stay at their studies until they could pass all the tests and get a certificate of registration.

My Father was quite a good engineer but after a time he broke away from Grandfather saying that Grandfather's control was too strict, too domineering. My Father went away to a different house still in St. Maurice but it was called Brick House because it was the only red brick house in that street. Father married and for a time lived in St. Maurice. First a son was born who shortly died, and then a daughter was born, and quite a time after I was born, and I have always believed that I was the unwanted accident, certainly I was never favoured in any way, I was never popular, never permitted to have friends. Everything I did was automatically wrong, everything my sister did was automatically right. It makes one rather disgruntled after a time to always be the unwanted one and to see the favourite get everything, to see her with her friends and her parties and all the rest of it. Even second best was considered to be too good for me.

Mother and Father moved to Ridgeway in the Parish of St. Mary. There they started a business—no, not plumbing —an engineering business which included electricity which was only then coming into popular use. My Father was a very nice man indeed so far as he could afford to be a very nice man. He was a Scorpio, and my Mother was a Virgo. She had come from an extremely good family in another part of Devonshire. The family had had a lot of money previously and a lot of land, but her father and a neighbour fell to quarrelling over a right-of-way, and—well—eventually they went to law. A verdict was given and was appealed, and so it went on until they had hardly any money left, certainly they had no money to continue litigation, and so the land which had been the cause of all the trouble was sold.

Mother and Father did not get on. Mother was too domineering, she was known locally as "The Lady" because of her high ambitions. She had been made very bitter by the loss of the family fortunes. Unfortunately she seemed to take her bitterness out on her husband and on me.

Grandfather had a brother who was a most talented artist, he was a Royal Academician and had made a very satisfactory name for himself. I remember one painting of his in particular always enthralled me. It was a picture of the Old Barbican, Plymouth; the Barbican as it was when the Mayflower sailed for the U.S.A. This was a wonderful picture, it glowed with living colour, it was mellow, and one could look at it and actually soon find that one was "there." Uncle Richard, as we called him, always said that that picture would go to one of us children. It did, to my sister and it is one thing which I really, really coveted, it was the thing that I wanted above all else except a few years later when I had been promised a model train—a blue train—and to my juvenile eyes it was the most wonderful train in the whole world, I had been solemnly promised it, and then on the day I was to have it I was told "Oh no, you can't have it. Your sister wants a piano. Your Father and I are going to get it now." Yes, I really wanted that train as I wanted the picture.

Things like that were always happening. My sister had a wonderful bicycle, I was left to walk. But that is not the purpose of this writing, I am having to tell all this because, I am told, it was part of the agreement when I consented to have my body taken over. I was sick of the damned body anyhow. It was all wrong.

I was born sickly, and my birth made my Mother very ill. She seemed to get some sort of poisoning when I was born, and for some strange reason it was held against me just as if I had poisoned her. There was nothing I could do about it, I was too young to know anything about it. Anyway she was very ill, so was I and I was ill all my life on Earth. I was sickly. We had a doctor, Dr. Duncan Stamp, he was one of the real doctors, always studying, always getting different letters after his name. He hadn't much sympathy, but he had plenty of knowledge. He didn't like me and I didn't like him. But I remember one extraordinary thing; one day I was—well, they said I was dying. This Dr. Stamp came along to my bed and he seemed to hang something up from a light fixture and run tubes down to me. To this day I don't know what he did, but I made a recovery, and I always thought of him after as the miracle worker.

I remember in the Great War, that is the First Great War. My parents and I and my sister were on North Road Station, Plymouth. We had had to visit somebody in an area called Penny-Come-Quick. It was late at night and suddenly we heard gunfire and searchlight beams flickered across the sky, and in the beam of searchlight I saw my first Zeppelin. It flew over Plymouth and then went out to sea again, but that is another incident I have never forgotten, how that ship looked in the crossed beams of light.

Plympton is an old old place full of history. There is the great church of St. Mary's at the foot of Church Hill. As one went down the hill the church spire seemed to be still higher than the top of the hill. One went down and went along by the churchyard, and then turned left. If one passed the church one came to the priory and various old religious houses, the use of which had been discontinued by the clergy because, apparently, some division of power had taken place and the head offices of the church had been removed to Buckfast.

Behind the priory there was a pleasant stream in which there were reeds and osiers. Here people used to get reeds and rushes for the making of baskets and other containers. Here, too, a hundred or so years before, they used to make mead which was the drink of the time.

The church was a most imposing place, of grey stone with a great tower with four little pillars at each corner of the tower. The bells were wonderful when properly played and campanologists used to come from all over Devon to ring the changes, as they called them, and the Plympton bell ringers used to go around in their turn showing their own skill.

St. Maurice church was not so grand as that of St. Mary. It was smaller and was obviously a satellite church. In those days St. Maurice and St. Mary's were separate communities with hardly any social movement between them. Colebrook and Underwood had no churches, they had instead to go to St. Maurice or St. Mary.

Plympton had its share of great houses, but most of them had been badly damaged by Oliver Cromwell and his men. Many of them had been demolished by the order of Judge Jeffreys, but Plympton Castle, that was a place that fascinated me. There was a great mound with the remnants of sturdy stone walls on it, and the walls were so thick, and some of us found that there was a tunnel going through the walls lengthwise. Some of the more hardy boys said they had been in to a strange chamber below the walls in which there were supposed to be skeletons, but I never got to be that venturesome, I just accepted their word. Plympton Castle stood on an amphitheatre, a big round space with a raised bank around it. The raised bank was a very nice place as a promenade, but the sunken piece in-between—as if in the centre of a saucer—was much used by circuses and other forms of public entertainment.

I was sent to my first school to a place called—of all unlikely names—Co-op Fields. It was so named because originally it was property owned by the Plympton Co-operative Wholesale Society. The land had been sold to raise funds for other development and a few houses had been built there, then a few more, and a few more, so that in the end it became a separate community, almost a small village on its own. And here I went to school. It was—well, I think it would be called a Dames School. It was a Miss Gillings and her sister. Together they ran what purported to be a school, but really it was more to keep

140

unruly children from plaguing their unwilling parents. The walk from Ridgeway right out to Miss Gillings school was a terrible ordeal for me in my sickly condition, but there was nothing I could do about it, I just had to go. After a time, though, I was considered to be too big to go to that school any longer so I was transferred to a Preparatory School. It was called Mr. Beard's school. Mr. Beard was a nice old man, a really clever old man, but he could not impose discipline.

He had retired from school life and then, getting bored with retirement, he had opened his own school, and the only premises he could find was a big room attached to the George Hotel. The George Hotel was at the top of George Hill and was quite well known. One entered under an archway and the ground was paved, and then to get to Mr. Beard's school one had to go all the way through the courtyard, past all the former stables and coach houses. At the far side of the yard there were wooden steps going up to a room which looked as if it had been an assembly hall. That was the first school where I started to learn anything, and I did not learn much, but that was my fault not the fault of old Beard. Actually, he was far too gentle to be a schoolmaster, people took advantage of him.

After a time the Plympton Grammar School reopened in a fresh location. Plympton Grammar School was one of the most famous Grammar Schools of England, many famous people had been there including Joshua Reynolds. In the old Grammar School in St. Maurice his name and the names of many other very famous people were carved into the desks and into the woodwork, but that school building had had to be closed down because the ravages of time had attacked the building and the upper floors were considered to be unsafe.

After a long search a very large house was secured which was in the shadow of Plympton Castle, in the shadow, actually, of that round part where the circuses used to come.

Vast sums were paid for its conversion, and I was one of the first pupils to be enrolled in that school. I didn't like

141

it a bit, I hated the place. Some of the teachers had been demobilised from the forces and instead of treating children as children they treated children as bloody-minded troops. One teacher in particular had a most vicious habit of breaking sticks of chalk in half and throwing each half with all his might at some offender, and although you might think that chalk couldn't do much damage I have seen a boy's face lascerated by the impact. Nowadays, I suppose the teacher would have gone to prison for bodily assault, but at least it kept us in order.

For recreation we had to go to the playing fields of the old Grammar School which gave us a walk of about a mile, a mile there, then all the exercise, etcetera, a mile back.

Eventually time came to leave school. I hadn't done anything too good but, then, I hadn't done anything too bad either. In addition to schoolwork I had to take some correspondence courses, and I got a few little bits of paper saying I was qualified in this, that, or something else. But when the time came to leave school my parents, without any such frivolities as asking me what I would like to be, apprenticed me to a motor engineering firm in Plymouth. So almost to the day on which I left school I was sent to this firm in Old Town Street, Plymouth. They sold a few cars, etcetera, but they were more concerned with motorcycles, in fact they were the South Devon agents for Douglas motorcycles. Again, it was an unsympathetic place because all that mattered was work. I used to leave Plympton early in the morning and travel by bus to Plymouth, five and a half miles away. By the time lunch time came I was famished, so whatever the weather I used to take my sandwiches—there was nothing to drink except water—and went to a little park at the back of St. Andrew's church, Plymouth. There I used to sit in the park and get my sandwiches down as fast as I could, otherwise I should have been late.

It was very very hard work indeed because sometimes we apprentices were sent out as far away as Crown Hill to fetch a heavy motorcycle. Well, we went to Crown Hill or

142

other places by bus—only one of us to one place, of course—and then we were faced with the problem of getting the blasted bikes back. We couldn't ride them because they were faulty, so the only ride we got was going downhill.

I remember one time I had to go to Crown Hill to fetch a very big Harley Davidson motorcycle. The owner had telephoned in and said the bike could be picked up right outside, so I went there, got off the bus, saw this motor bike, pushed it off its stand and pushed it away. I had done about three miles when a police car pulled up right in front of me. Two policemen got out and I thought they were going to kill me! One grabbed me by the neck, the other grabbed my arms behind me, and all so suddenly that the bike tipped over and bruised my shins. The bike was propped up by the side of the road and I was bundled into the back of the police car and whisked off to Crown Hill Police Station. Here a shouting Police sergeant threatened me with all manner of terrible deaths unless I told him who were my fellow gangsters.

Now, I wasn't very old at this time and I just didn't know what he was talking about, so he gave me a few cuffs about the ears and then put me in a cell. He wouldn't listen to my explanation that I had come to fetch a motorcycle as instructed.

About eight hours later one of the men from the firm came and identified me, and confirmed that I had been quite legitimately collecting a faulty motor bike. The police sergeant gave me a cuff across the face and told me not to get in trouble again and not to bother them. So I don't like policemen, I have had trouble with police all through my life, and I would swear this: Never have I done anything which warrants police persecution. Each time it has just been police slovenliness, such as that time when they wouldn't let me explain what had happened.

The next day, though, the owner of the bike came into the firm and laughed like a maniac. He was quite unsympathetic, he didn't seem to think what a shock it was to be hauled off and taken to a police cell.

One day I could hardly get out of bed, I felt ill, I felt so ill I just wanted to die. It was no good, my Mother insisted on getting me out of bed. So eventually I had to go without any breakfast, the day was wet and the day was cold. She went with me to the bus stop and shoved me on the old Devon Motor Transport bus so roughly that I fell to my knees.

I got to work, but after about two hours there I fainted and somebody said I ought to be taken home, but the man in charge said they didn't have time to run around after apprentices in trouble, so I was kept there until the end of the day, no breakfast, no lunch, nothing.

At the end of the working day I made my way most dizzily along the street toward the bus stop in front of St. Andrew's church. Fortunately there was a bus waiting and I collapsed into a corner seat. When I got home I just had enough strength to totter into bed. There wasn't much interest in my welfare, nobody asked how I was feeling, nobody asked why I couldn't eat my dinner, I just went off to bed.

I had a terrible night, I felt I was on fire and I was wet through with perspiration. In the morning my Mother came along and awakened me quite roughly—for I had fallen into an exhausted sleep—and even she could see that I wasn't well. Eventually she phoned Dr. Stamp. Half a day later he came. He took one look at me and said, "Hospital!" So the ambulance came—in those days the ambulance was run by the local undertaker—and I was taken off to the South Devon and East Cornwall Hospital. I had very bad lung trouble.

I stayed in that hospital for about eleven weeks, and then there was great discussion as to whether I should be sent to a Sanatorium or not because I'd got T.B.

Father and Mother were opposed to it because, they said, they wouldn't have time to come and visit me if I was sent to a Sanatorium a few miles away. So I stayed at home and I didn't get much better. Every so often I had to go back to hospital. Then my sight went wrong and I was taken to the Royal Eye Infirmary, Mutley Plain, which wasn't so far from the South Devon and East Cornwall Hospital. This was quite a pleasant hospital, if one can say anything is pleasant when one is blind. But eventually I was released from the hospital with greatly impaired sight and I went home again.

By now wireless was well known—it used to be wireless before radio. My Father had a crystal set and I thought it was the most marvellous thing I had ever seen in my life. Father studied a lot about radio and he made vast radio sets with many valves to them, and then he set up in business building radio sets for people and doing electrical work for people.

At this time it was decided I should go away for a change, and so, as sick as I was, I was put on an old bicycle and sent with a workman to Lydford where I had an aunt. I often wished that this aunt had been my mother. She was a very good woman indeed, and I loved her as I certainly did not love my Mother. She looked after me, she really treated me as if I were one of her own children, but, as she said, its not much to have a sick child ride twenty-five miles when he can hardly draw breath. But eventually I had to return home and the journey was much easier this time. Lydford is up in the Devonshire moors, up in Dartmoor beyond Tavistock, not too far from Okehampton, and the air was pure there and the food good.

Back at home in Plympton I started studying other correspondence courses, and then my Mother told me I ought to work. So my Father had a lot of radio sets and electrical stuff so I had to travel about selling the things to small dealers. I went all along Elburton, Modbury, Okehampton, and other places like that selling accumulators, radio parts, and electrical stuff. But after a time the very very harried life proved to be too much for me and my health broke down. I was driving a car at that time, and I went blind. Now, it is a thoroughly unpleasant thing to lose one's sight completely and utterly when driving. Fortunately I was able to stop the car without any damage and I just stayed where I was until somebody came to see

145

what was happening and why I was blocking traffic. For a time I couldn't convince people that I was ill and that I couldn't see, but eventually the police were called and they had me taken by ambulance to hospital. My parents were informed and their first thought was about the car. When the car was driven home it was found that all the stuff I had had in it was stolen, radio sets, batteries, test equipment, everything. So I was not popular. But a spell in hospital put me right for a time, and then I went home again.

I studied some more and eventually it was decided that I should try to get training as a radio operator. So I went to Southampton and outside Southampton there was a special school which trained one to be radio operator aboard aircraft. I stayed there for some time, and passed my examinations and got a licence as a first-class wireless operator. I had to go to Croydon to take the examination, and I was successful. At the same time I learned to fly aircraft and managed to get a license at that as well. But— I could not pass the medical examination for a commercial licence and so I was grounded before my career started.

Back at home I was blamed quite a lot for having bad health and for wasting money in taking these courses when my health was so poor that I had been rejected. I felt a bit irritated by that because I was not to blame for my bad health, I didn't want to be ill. But there was a big family conference and my parents decided something would have to be done, I was just wasting my life.

At that identical moment the local sanitary inspector who was very friendly with my parents said there was a great opening for smoke inspectors, particularly in the big cities, people were getting worried about the ecology and there was too much smoke pollution from factories and industrial concerns so a new category of smoke inspectors had been started. There were, of course, sanitary inspectors and sanitary inspectors who were meat inspectors, but now there was a new category—smoke inspectors. The chief sanitary inspector said it would be just the thing for

146

me, it was a good job, well paid, and I would have to take a special course, naturally. So a new correspondence course had just been brought out for smoke inspectors. I studied it at home and passed very quickly, in three months actually, and then I was told I would have to go to London to study with the Royal Sanitary Institute in Buckingham Palace Road. So not too happily my parents advanced the money and I went to London. Every day I attended classes at the Royal Sanitary Institute, and often we went out on field trips going to factories, power stations, and all manner of queer places. At last, after three months, we had to go to an immense examination hall where there seemed to be thousands of people milling around. We were all in little groups; one who was going to take a particular examination would be isolated from others taking the same type of examination. Anyway, I passed the examination and got a certificate as a smoke inspector.

I returned to Plympton bearing my certificate and thinking that now everything would be plain sailing. But it was not to be. I applied for a job in Birmingham, and I went to Birmingham—to Lozelles—for interview. There I was told that I couldn't get the job because I was not a resident of that county.

Back to Plympton I went and tried for a job in Plymouth. But the Plymouth city council would not employ me for much the same reason except I was in the right county, but not in the right city. So it went on, and after a few years like this in which I did anything that I could do—anything to bring in enough money to keep body and soul together and to keep me in some sort of clothing—my Father died. He had been in very poor health for years. Most of the time he had been in bed, and about a year before he died his business had been sold off and the shop had been made into a doctor's surgery. The glass windows were painted green and the shop itself was the surgery with our living part being used as the consulting room and dispensary. My Mother and I lived in what had been our workrooms.

But after Father's death the doctor-combine decided to move to a fresh area and so we would have no income at all. My health was not at all good, so my Mother went to her daughter, my sister, and I had been a prize student of a correspondence college so I got a job with a surgical appliance firm in Perivale, Middlesex. I was appointed first as works manager, but when the owner of the firm found that I could write good advertising copy then he made me advertising manager as well.

I had to take courses in surgical fitting, and after that I became a surgical fitter consultant.

I was considered so good at this work that I was moved from Perivale to the heart of London, and I was the chief fitter in the London offices.

Just before I left work at the London offices war was declared between England and Germany. Everything was blacked out and I found the journey to London from Perivale and back every day to be absolutely exhausting, it tried my strength to the utmost, and during this time I got married. Well, I do not propose to say anything about this because I understand that the press on Earth have already said too much, nearly all of it untrue. I have been asked to talk about my life, so I will confine myself strictly to my life.

We could not continue to live in Perivale because conditions in travelling were too bad, so we managed to find an apartment in the Knightsbridge area of London. It was a blessing to be able to go on the tube every day to my office.

The war was hotting up, things were becoming difficult, there was heavy rationing and food shortages. Bombs were dropping heavily on London. Much of my time was spent on fire watch, I had to climb rusty iron ladders going to the top of buildings and watch out for approaching German bombers, and if I saw them in time I had to give warning to the work people below.

One day I was riding through Hyde Park on my bicycle going to work and I saw bombers approaching. One dropped bombs which seemed as if they were going to

148

come uncomfortably close to me, so I dropped my bicycle and ran for some trees. The bombs fell, they missed the Park and landed in Buckingham Palace where they did a fair amount of damage.

Everywhere, it seemed, bombs were dropping. One day I was having to go out on a special surgical fitting case and was approaching Charing Cross Station when suddenly a great bomb dropped out of the clouds, went into the station and right through the station to the Underground which was crowded with people. I can see even now the cloud of dust and scattered pieces of—what?— that were blown out of the hole in the station roof.

One night there was a terrific air raid and the place where my wife and I lived was bombed. We had to get out in the night just as we were. For a long time we wandered about in the darkness, other people were wandering about as well, everything was chaotic. Bombs were dropping and the sky was lurid with the flames of the burning East End. We could see St. Paul's Cathedral outlined in flame and great clouds of smoke went up. Every so often we would hear the rat-tat-tat of machine-gun fire, and occasionally spent cartridges would fall down around us. Everywhere there was shrapnel falling and we wore our steel helmets because the smoking fragments hurtling down would have gone through an unprotected body.

At last the dawn came and I phoned my employer to say that I had been bombed out. He said, "Never mind about that, you must come to work. Other people are bombed out too. So, dirty and hungry, I got on a train and went to my office. At the approach of our street there I found that it was cordoned off. I tried to go past the barrier but a most officious policeman came up and accused me of looting—tempers were quite rough at that time. Just at that moment my boss stepped out of a car and came up to me. He showed his identification papers to the policeman and together we crossed the barrier and went to our office.

Water was rushing out of everywhere. The place had been hit by a bomb and the water supply had been broken

149

to shards. From the roof, many floors above, water was cascading over the stock. The basement was neck-deep in water and everywhere there was glass, everywhere there were stone fragments, and we turned and found a bomb casing lodged in a wall.

It was a state of chaos. There was not much worth saving. We managed to get out some records and just a few pieces of equipment and we all set to and tried to clean up the place a bit, but it was hopeless—there was no chance of getting the place working again. Eventually my employer said he was going to move to another part of the country, and he invited me to accompany him. I could not do so because I hadn't the money. It was very difficult indeed to buy things, and to have to set up a fresh home in some remote part of the country was an expense which I just could not contemplate. So—because I was unable to go I was out of a job, unemployed in England in wartime.

I went to various labour exchanges trying to get any employment. I tried to become a wartime policeman, but I could not pass the medical examination. Conditions were becoming desperate; one cannot live on air, and as a last resort I went to the offices of the correspondence school where I had taken so many courses.

It just so happened that they wanted a man, some of their own men had been called up, and I had—so I was told—an enviable record, and so I was told that I could be given a job in the advisory department. The pay would be five pounds a week, and I would have to live at Weybridge in Surrey. No, they said, they couldn't advance anything to help me get there. I would have to go there first for interview with one of the directors. So I made inquiries and found that the cheapest way was by Green Line Bus, so on the appointed day I went to Weybridge but there was a terrific wait, the director had not come in. I was told, "Oh, he never comes in the time he says, he might not be in until four o'clock. You'll just have to wait." Well, eventually the director did come in, he saw me and he was quite affable, and he offered me the job at five pounds a week. He told me there was an unoccupied flat over the garage and I could have this by paying what was really quite a high rent, but I was in a hurry to get employment so I agreed to his terms. I returned to London and we got our poor things, such as they were, to Weybridge, up the worn old wooden steps to the flat above the garages. The next day I started my work as a correspondence clerk, which is what it really was, to a correspondence school.

There are such a lot of high falutin terms; we now have garbage collectors called sanitation experts when all they are is garbage collectors. Some of the correspondence clerks call themselves advisory consultants or careers consultants, but still all we did was correspondence clerks' duties.

It seems to be a crime to be of a certain category. I have always been told that my Father was a plumber; actually, he wasn't, but what if he had been? Certainly he served an apprenticeship as a plumber but, like me, he had no choice. I served an apprenticeship as a motor engineer. And anyway, how about the famous Mr. Crapper, the gentleman who invented water closets as they are today? They have not been improved since the day of old Crapper. Crapper, if you remember, was a plumber, a jolly good one, too, and his invention of the flush tank and the flush toilet endeared him to King Edward who treated Mr. Crapper as a personal friend. So, you see, a plumber can be a friend of royalty just as can a grocer; Thomas Lipton was alleged to be a grocer. Certainly he was, he had a big grocery firm, and he was a friend of King George V. Surely it doesn't matter what a person's father was, why is it such a disgrace to have a parent who was a tradesman? Nowadays daughters of royalty are married to tradesmen, aren't they? But I am always amused because Jesus, it is said, was the son of a carpenter. How was that a disgrace?

Well, all this is taking me a long way from my story, but I will just say here and now that I would rather be the son of a plumber than the son of those poor sick people who call themselves pressmen. To me there is no sicker job than that of pressman. A plumber clears up the messes of people. A pressman makes messes of people.

Since I have been over here I have found various things of interest, but one thing in particular which intrigues me is this; I bear quite an honoured name not merely through "Uncle Richard" but through others who went before him, one who was a colleague of Sir Joshua Reynolds, and another was the Lord Lieutenant, or whatever they call him, of the Tower of London. And it was at the time when an attempt was made to steal the Crown Jewels, an attempt which was thwarted.

There is much to see over here, much to learn, and I am told I have a lot yet to learn because, they say, I have not learned humility, not yet learned how to get on with people. Well, I am doing my best in dictating all this stuff which I will swear upon a stack of Bibles is the truth and nothing but the truth.

CHAPTER NINE

Life at Weybridge was not happy. I became an air raid warden. One other warden became very jealous and did everything he could to cause me harm. I offered to resign but it was not wanted for me to resign.

One night there was an air raid while I was at Weybridge and after the air raid a policeman came to the door. It seemed that a small light—hardly large enough for anyone to notice from a hundred feet away—was showing. There was a faulty switch in the flat, on the landing, it was one of those old brass switches with a great knob, and I suppose the vibration caused by the banging and all that, had shaken it just to the "on" position. The policeman could see for himself that if a fly sneezed the light would come on because the spring in the tumbler was defective. But, no, the light was showing, that's all there was to it. So there was a Court appearance and a fine. And that is a thing I have resented ever since because it was so utterly unnecessary, and "the enemy" warden was the one who had reported it. After that I resigned from the A.R.P. believing that if people could not work together then it was better to break us "the party."

At Weybridge I was supposed to do everything, answer letters, persuade people to take correspondence courses, maintain the boss's cars—and he was always changing the darn things—act as unpaid messenger boy and do anything which came to hand. All for five pounds a week!

People were getting called-up, conditions were becoming more difficult, food was getting shorter and shorter, and from the aircraft factory at Brooklands there were always strange noises. One day a Wellington was being flight-tested and it crashed just beside the village of Weybridge. The pilot saved the village at the cost of his own life because he crashed that plane upon the electrified railway line. The plane was like a toy that had been snapped into a thousand pieces, it was scattered all over the place, but the people of Weybridge were saved because of the self-sacrifice of the pilot.

Just at this time I received my call-up papers. I had to go before a Board of Medical Examiners as a formality before entering one of the Services.

On the appointed day I went to the great hall where there were crowds of other men waiting to be examined. I said to an attendant there, "I've had T.B., you know." He looked at me and said, "You look a bit of a wreck, I must say lad. Sit over there." So I sat where directed, and I sat, and I sat. Eventually when nearly everyone else in the place had been examined, the panel of doctors turned to me. "What's this?" said one, "You say you've got T.B. Do you know what T.B. is?" "I certainly do, sir," I said. "I've had it." He asked me a lot of questions and then grumphed and grumphed. Then he had a word with his associates. At last he turned back to me as if he was making the greatest decision in the world.

"I am sending you to Kingston Hospital," he said. "They will examine you there, they will soon find out if you've got T.B. or not, and if you haven't—God help you!" He carefully filled out a form, sealed it, put it in another envelope and sealed that, and then flung it at me. I picked it off the floor and made my way home.

Next day I told my employer that I had to go to hospital for examination. He appeared absolutely bored, I got the impression that he thought, "Oh why does the fellow waste my time, why doesn't he join up and get out of my sight." However, I got through my work that day, and the day after, as directed, I took the bus to Kingston-on-Thames. I made my way to a hospital there. I had all sorts of tests and then I was X-rayed. After the X-ray I was shoved in a drying cupboard where a lot of wet X-rays were hung up to dry out. After half an hour a woman came and said, "Okay, you can go home!" That was all, nothing more was said, so I just went home.

Next there came a summons to go to the T.B. Clinic at Weybridge. Of course, this was about three or four weeks later, but the summons came and off I went to the T.B. Clinic like a good little boy. By now I was heartily sick of the whole affair. At the T.B. Clinic I was seen by a most wonderful doctor who was indeed all that a doctor should be. He had my X-rays there, and he agreed with me that it was utterly stupid that I should be shunted from one department to another. He said it was perfectly obvious that I had bad lung scars through T.B., and, he said if I got in the Army I would be a liability, not an asset. Surely England hadn't come to a state when they are called upon to enlist those who are obviously ill. "I shall send a report in to say that you are unfitted for service of any kind," he said.

Time went by, and at last I received a card in the post telling me that I would not be required for military service because I was classed as Grade Four—the lowest grade there was.

I took the card to my employer and showed it to him, and he seemed to think that—well, he'd got somebody to carry on with the work if all the others were called up. There was a frantic scramble in those days of people trying to get deferment, everybody was trying to get deferment.

154

The man who was manager under the employer left to get another job and another man was appointed as manager, but he and I didn't get on at all, we just did not get on at all. He was of a type that I thoroughly disliked and I seemed to be of a type that he thoroughly disliked. However, I did the best I could, but things were becoming more and more difficult because there was more and more work without any increase in pay. It was obvious that someone was rushing around to the employer telling tales, etcetera, not necessarily true tales either.

One day after work I was just meandering through the garden. We had a garden of three and a half acres and I was passing through a little wooded copse. It was evening and growing dusk. Somehow I tripped over an exposed root and went down with a horrible thonk. Literally it jerked me out of myself!

I stood upright, but then—God bless my soul! I found that "I" wasn't "me" because I was standing upright and my body was lying flat on its face. I looked about in utter amazement, and I saw some strange looking people around me. Monks, I thought, what the devil are monks doing here? I looked at them, and I looked at—well, I suppose it was my body on the ground. But then I got a voice or something in my head. First I had the impression that it was some strange foreign lingo, but as I thought about it I discovered that I could understand what was being said.

"Young man," the voice said in my head, "you are thinking of an evil matter, you are thinking of doing away with your life. That is a very bad thing indeed. Suicide is wrong, no matter the cause, no matter the imagined reason or excuse, suicide is always wrong."

"All right for you," I thought, "you haven't any troubles like I have. Here I am in this—well, I had an awful job not to put in words the exact description of the place —and I can't get a rise, and my boss seems to have taken a dislike to me, why should I stay here? There are plenty of trees about and a nice rope to throw over."

But I am not saying too much about this because a

thought was put in my mind saying that if I wanted to I could get release from what I considered to be the tortures of Earth. If I wanted to, if I was really serious, I could do something for mankind by making my body available to some ghost or spirit which wanted to hop in almost before I had hopped out. It seemed a lot of rubbish to me, but I thought I would give it a whirl and let them talk on. First, they said, as a sign of genuine interest, I had to change my name. They told me a strange name they wanted me to adopt, but—well, I told my wife only that I was going to change my name, she thought I was a bit mad or something and let it go at that, and so I did change my name quite legally.

Then my teeth started giving trouble. I had a horrible time. At last I couldn't stick it any longer and I went to a local dentist. He made an attempt to extract the tooth but it wouldn't come. He made a hole in the thing so he could use an elevator—not the type people use to travel to different floors, but the type which is meant to elevate a tooth by leverage. This dentist got on the phone to some specialist in London, and I had to go to a nursing home in a hurry.

My wife told my employer that I had to go to a nursing home, and she was met with the statement, "Well, I have to work when I have toothache!" And that was all the sympathy we got. So I went to this nursing home, at my own expense, of course, there was no such thing as health schemes like you seem to have now, and I had this little operation which was not so easy after all. The dentist was good, the anaesthetist was even better. I stayed in the nursing home a week and then returned to Weybridge.

There were quite a number of unpleasant little incidents, needlings and all that sort of thing, and unjust accusations. There is no point in going into all the details, raking up muck, because, after all, I am not a pressman. But there were false accusations, so my wife and I talked it over and we decided that we couldn't stick it any longer, so I handed in my notice. From that moment I might have been a leper, or I might have had an even worse form of plague, because for the rest of the week I sat in my office, no one came to see me, they apparently had been told not to, and no work of any kind was given to me. I just stayed there like a convict serving out time. At the end of the week that was it, I was finished.

We left Weybridge with joy and we went to London. We moved about a bit, oh gracious, I forget how many places we tried, and anyway it doesn't matter, but then we found that conditions were intolerable and we moved on to another place, a suburb of London called Thames Ditton.

Oh, I am so anxious to get this silly affair over because I do not enjoy talking about this, but I was in such a hurry that I have forgotten one bit. Here it is: I had been told sometime before that I would have to grow a beard. Well, I thought, what's it matter? Just as well be hung for a sheep as a lamb, so while I was at Weybridge I grew this beard and was jeered at quite a bit by my employer and by those who worked with me. Never mind, I thought, I wouldn't be with them much longer.

We moved to Thames Ditton; for a very short time we stayed in a lodging house which was run by a funny old woman who just could not see dirt. She thought she lived in a ducal mansion, or something, and was quite incapable of seeing immense cobwebs high up in the corners of the stairway. But she was too ladylike and so we looked for another place. Down the road there was such a place, a house which was being rented as an upper and lower flat. We took the place, we had no thought of how we were going to get money because I had no job, no job at all. Instead I was just doing anything to earn odd bits of money to keep us alive. I went to the Unemployment Exchange but because I had left my employment instead of being fired I was not able to get any unemployment benefit. So that never have I had any unemployment money, I managed without, to this day I don't know how, but I did.

I had an old bicycle and I used to ride around trying to get work, but no, no work was available. The war had ended, men had come back from the Forces, and the labour market was saturated. It was all right for them, they had unemployment benefit and perhaps a pension; I had nothing.

Then one night I was approached by a group of men. They hoiked me out of my body, and talked to me, and they asked me if I still wanted to get out of my body into what I then thought was Paradise. I suppose it is Paradise, but these people called it the astral world. I assured them I wanted to get out even more than before, so they told me that the very next day I must stay at home. One man, he was all done up in a yellow robe, took me to the window and pointed out. He said, "That tree—you must go to that tree and put your hands up on that branch, and go to pull yourself up and then let go." He gave me the exact time at which I must do this, telling me it was utterly vital to follow instructions to the letter, otherwise I would have a lot of pain, and so would other people. But worse, for me—I would still be left on the Earth.

The next day my wife thought I had gone bonkers or something because I didn't go out as usual, I pottered about. And then a minute or two before the appointed time I went out into the garden and walked over to the tree. I pulled on a branch of ivy, or whatever it is that ivy has, and reached up to the branch as directed. And then I felt as if I had been struck by lightning. I had no need to pretend to fall, I did fall—whack down! I fell down, and then, good gracious me, I saw a silver rope sticking out of me. I went to grab it to see what it was but gently my hands were held away. I lay there on the ground feeling horribly frightened because two people were at that silver rope, and they were doing something to it, and a third person was there with another silver rope in his hand, and, horror of horrors, I could see through the whole bunch of them, so I wondered if I was seeing all this or if I had dashed my brains out, it was all so strange.

At last there was a sucking sort of noise and a plop, and then I found—oh joy of joy—I was floating free in a beautiful, beautiful world, and that means that having gone so far I fulfilled my part of the contract, I have said all I am going to about my past life, and now I am going back to my own part of the astral world. . . .

I am Lobsang Rampa, and I have finished transcribing that which was so unwillingly, so ungraciously, told to me by the person whose body I took over. Let me continue where he left off.

His body was upon the ground, twitching slightly, and I—well, I confess without too much shame, that I was twitching also but my twitches were caused by fright. I didn't like the look of this body stretched out there in front of me, but a lama of Tibet follows orders, pleasant orders as well as unpleasant ones, so I stood by while two of my brother lamas wrestled with the man's Silver Cord. They had to attach mine before his was quite disconnected. Fortunately the poor fellow was in an awful state of daze and so he was quiescent.

At last, after what seemed hours but actually was only about a fifth of a second, they got my Silver Cord attached and his detached. Quickly he was led away, and I looked at that body to which I was now attached and shuddered. But then, obeying orders, I let my astral form sink down on that body which was going to be mine. Ooh, the first contact was terrible, cold, slimy. I shot off in the air again in fright. Two lamas came forward to steady me, and gradually I sank again.

Again I made contact, and I shivered with horror and repulsion. This truly was an incredible, a shocking experience, and one that I never want to undergo again.

I seemed to be too large, or the body seemed to be too small. I felt cramped, I felt I was being squeezed to death, and the smell! The difference! My old body was tattered and dying, but at least it had been my own body. Now I was stuck in this alien thing and I didn't like it a bit.

Somehow—and I cannot explain this—I fumbled about inside trying to get hold of the motor nerves of the brain. How did I make this confounded thing work? For a time I lay there just helpless, just as if I were paralysed. The body would not work. I seemed to be fumbling like an inexperienced driver with a very intricate car. But at last with the help of my astral brothers I got control of myself. I managed to make the body work. Shakily I got to my feet, and nearly screamed with horror as I found that I was walking backwards instead of forwards. I teetered and fell again. It was indeed a horrendous experience. I was truly nauseated by this body and was in fear that I should not be able to manage it.

I lay upon my face on the ground and just could not move, then from the corner of an eye I saw two lamas standing by looking highly concerned at the difficulty I was having. I growled, "Well, you try it for yourself, see if you can make this abominable thing do what you tell it to do!"

Suddenly one of the lamas said, "Lobsang! Your fingers are twitching, now try with your feet." I did so, and found that there was an amazing difference between Eastern and Western bodies. I never would have thought such a thing possible, but then I remembered something I had heard while a ship's Engineer; for ships in Western waters the propeller should rotate in one direction, and for Eastern waters it should rotate in the opposite direction. It seems clear to me, I said to myself, that I've got to start out all over again. So I kept calm and let myself lift out of the body, and from the outside I looked at it carefully. The more I looked at it the less I liked it, but then, I thought, there was nothing for it but to try once again. So again I squeezed uncomfortably into the slimy, cold thing which was a Western body.

With immense effort I tried to rise, but fell again, and then at last I managed to scramble somehow to my feet and pressed my back against that friendly tree.

There was a sudden clatter from the house and a door was flung open. A woman came running out saying, "Oh! What have you done now. Come in and lie down." It gave me quite a shock. I thought of those two lamas with me and I was fearful that the woman might throw a fit at the sight of them, but obviously they were completely invisible to her, and that again was one of the surprising things of

160

my life. I could always see these people who visited me from the astral, but if I talked to them and then some other person came in—well, the other person thought I was talking to myself and I didn't want to get the reputation of being off my head.

The woman came toward me and as she looked at me a very startled expression crossed her face. I really thought she was going to get hysterical but she controlled herself somehow and put an arm across my shoulders.

Silently I thought of how to control the body and then very slowly, thinking a step at a time, I made my way into the house and went up the stairs, and flopped upon what was obviously my bed.

For three whole days I remained in that room pleading indisposition while I practised how to make the body do what I wanted it to do, and trying to contain myself because this was truly the most frightening experience I had had in my life. I had put up with all manner of torments in China and in Tibet and in Japan, but this was a new and utterly revolting experience, the experience of being imprisoned in the body of another person and having to control it.

I thought of that which I had been taught so many years ago, so many years ago that indeed it seemed to be a different life. "Lobsang," I had been told, "in the days of long ago the Great Beings from far beyond this system and Beings who were not in human form, had to visit this Earth for special purposes. Now, if they came in their own guise they would attract too much attention, so always they had bodies ready which they could enter and control, and appear to be the natives of the place. In the days to come," I was told, "you will have such an experience, and you will find it to be utterly shocking."

I did!

For the benefit of those who are genuinely interested let me say a few things about transmigration because really I have so much to tell the world, and yet because of the vilification of the press people have been hocussed into disbelieving my story. I will tell you more about that in the next Book, but one of the things I was going to do was to show people how transmigration worked because there are so many advantages to it. Think of this, which I am going to put to you as a definite possibility; mankind has sent a messenger to the Moon, but mankind does not know how to travel in deep space. In relation to the distances in the Universe the journey to the Moon pales into utter insignificance.It would take many millions of years for a space ship to travel to some other stars, and yet there is a much simpler way, and I say to you absolutely definitely that astral travel could be that way. It has been done before, it is being done now by creatures (I say "creatures" because they are not in human form) who come from a completely different galaxy. They are here now at this moment, they have come by astral travel, and some of them occupy human bodies such as did the Ancients of Old.

Humans, if they knew how, could send astral travellers anywhere transcending time and space. Astral travel can be as quick as thought, and if you don't know how quick thought is I will tell you—it would take a tenth of a second to go from here to Mars by astral travel. But in days to come explorers will be able to go to a world by astral travel and there, by transmigration, they will be able to enter the body of a native of that world so that they may gain first hand experience of what things are like. Now, this is not science fiction. It is absolutely true. If other people on other worlds can do it, then Earth people can do it also. But sadly I have to say that purely because of the false doubt which has been cast upon my word this particular aspect has not been able to be taught to people.

Unfortunately when one takes over a body there are certain grave disabilities. Let me give you an illustration; I found soon after I had taken over a body that I could not write Sanskrit, I could not write Chinese. Oh yes, definitely I knew the language, I knew what I should be writing, but—the body which I inhabited was not "geared" for making those squiggles which are Sanskrit or Chinese. It was only able to reproduce, say, letters such as English, French, German or Spanish.

162

It is all to do with muscular control. You have had the same things even in the West when you find that a well educated German with a better education than most English, let us say, still cannot pronounce English as the natives do. He cannot "get his tongue around" the sounds. So no matter how highly he is educated he still cannot say the sounds correctly. It is said almost universally that you can always tell if a man is a native of a district or not by the manner in which he pronounces his words, that is, can he manage his vocal chords as the native would, or does habit bring in certain disonances which the native lacks.

In transferring to a different body one can do all the sounds, etcetera, because the body is producing sounds to which it is accustomed, English, French or Spanish, for example. But when it comes to writing that is a different matter.

Look at it this way; some people can draw or they can paint. So let us say that these people—the artists—have an ability to produce certain squiggles which have a definite meaning. Now, most people, even of the same race, cannot do that, and even with training—even with immense practise—unless a person is a "born artist" the art forms are not considered acceptable. The same type of thing happens when an Eastern entity takes over a Western body. He can communicate in speech and he can know all that could be done in writing, but no longer can he write in that which was his original language such as Sanskrit or Chinese or Japanese because it takes years of practise, and his attempts are so fumbling, so crude, that the ideographs have no intelligible meaning.

Another difficulty is that the entity is Eastern and the body or vehicle is Western. If you find that strange let me say that if you were in England you would be driving a car with right hand controls so that you may drive on the left hand side of the road, but if you are in America you drive a car in which the steering wheel is on the left hand side, and then you drive on the right hand side of the road. Everyone knows that, eh? Well, you take some poor wretch of a driver who has been used to driving along the

163

lanes of England, suddenly lift him out and put the poor soul slap into an American car and without any teaching at all let him loose on the American roads. The poor fellow wouldn't have much chance, would he? He wouldn't last long. All his built-in reflexes which may have been trained for half a lifetime would scream at having to be reversed suddenly, and in the emergency he would immediately drive to the wrong side of the road and cause the accident which he was trying to avoid. Do you follow that clearly? Believe me, I know this, it all happened to me. So transmigration is not for the uninitiated. I say in all sincerity, there could be a lot done in transmigration if people could get the right knowledge, and I am surprised that the Russians who are so far ahead in so many things have not yet hit upon the idea of transmigration. It is easy—if you know how. It is easy—if you can have suitable precautions. But if you try to teach these things, as I could, and you have a lot of mindless children, or press people, then the whole thing becomes negated almost before one can start.

Another point which has to be considered is obtaining a suitable vehicle or body, because you cannot just jump into any body and take over like a bandit entering a car stopped at a traffic light. Oh no, it is much harder than that. You have to find a body which is harmonious to your own, which has a harmonic somewhere, and it doesn't mean to say that the owner of the body has to be good or bad, that has nothing to do with it at all; it is to do with the vibrational frequency of that body.

If you are interested in radio you will know that you can have, let us say, a super-heterodyne receiver which has three tuning condensers. Now if the set is working properly you get one station clearly, but as you get on harmonics you actually pick up the same signal on different wavelengths or different frequencies—it is all the same thing. In a frequency one just counts the number of times the wave changes from positive to negative, etcetera. But when you take a wavelength you just measure the distance between adjacent wave-crests. It is the same as calling a rose by another name, but what I am trying to tell you is that if you know how, transmigration is possible. Not only is it possible, but it is going to be an everyday thing in the distant future here on Earth.

But back to Thames Ditton. It was quite a nice little place, one of the suburbias of the great city of London. I believe it is also called one of the dormitories of London. There were a number of trees in the place, and every morning one could see businessmen scurrying away to Thames Ditton station where they would get a train taking them to Wimbledon and other parts of London so they could do their daily work. Many of the men were from the City of London, stockbrokers, insurance men, bankers, and all the rest of it. Where I lived was right opposite the Cottage Hospital. Much further on to the right one came to a sort of sports ground, and adjacent to the sports ground was a big building called the Milk Marketing Board.

Thames Ditton was "better class" and some of the voices I could hear through my open window were too much "better class" because I found some of the heavily accented voices difficult indeed to understand.

But speech was not easy for me. I had to think before I could utter a sound, and then I had to visualise the shape of the sound I was trying to say. Speech to most people comes naturally. You can babble forth without any difficulty, without any great thought, but not when you are an Easterner who has taken over a Western body. Even to this day I have to think what I am going to say, and that makes my speech appear somewhat slow and at times hesitant.

If one takes over a body, for the first year or two the body is basically the body of the host, that is, it was taken over. But in the course of time the body frequency changes and eventually it becomes of the same frequency as one's original body, and one's original scars appear. It is, as I told you before, like electro-plating or like electro-typing because molecule changes for molecule. This should not be too difficult to believe because if you get a cut and the cut heals then you've got replacement molecules, haven't you? They are not the same molecules that were cut but new cells that were grown to replace the cut ones. It is something like that in transmigration. The body ceases to be the alien body taken over, instead molecule by molecule it becomes one's own body, the body which one has grown.

Just one last piece of information about transmigration. It makes one "different." It gives associates a peculiar feeling to be close to one, and if a transmigrated person touches another person unexpectedly that other person may squeak with shock and say, "Oh now you've given me goose pimples!" So if you want to practise transmigration you will have to consider the disadvantages as well as the advantages. You know how strange dogs sniff around each other, stiff-legged, waiting for the first move by the other? Well, that is how I have found people in the Western world toward me. They do not understand me, they don't know what it is all about, they feel that there is something different and they do not know what it is, so often they will have uncertainty about me. They do not know if they like me or if they thoroughly dislike me, and it really does make difficulties, difficulties which are made manifest in the way that policemen are always suspicious of me, customs officials are always ready to believe the worst, and immigration officers always want to inquire further as to why, how, and when, etcetera, etcetera. It makes one, in effect, unacceptable to "the local natives." But we must get on to the next Book, but before we do here is a final word in case you find it difficult to understand that which I have written about Easterners who have transmigrated being able to write their own language; if you are right-handed write this paragraph with your right hand, then try to do the same thing with your left!

So ends the third Book
The Book of Changes.

166

BOOK FOUR

As it is Now!

CHAPTER TEN

Sunlight glanced off the placid river sailing so majestically by, sweeping along down to the sea like the Akashic Record sweeping along down to the sea of Universal Knowledge. But here THIS river was engaging my attention. I looked through half-closed eyes at all the little sparklets, at the dappled surface as occasionally a leaf went floating by. There was a sudden rustle and flutter, and three water birds alighted with great splashing on the surface of the water. For some moments they splashed around, throwing water over themselves, digging beneath their wings and generally having a good avian time. Then, as if at a sudden signal, they spread their wings, paddled their feet and took off in formation leaving three increasing circles of ripples behind them.

Sunlight through the leaves of the trees put contrasting spots of light and shadow on the waters edge before me. The sun was warm. I lay back and became aware of a buzzing noise. Slowly I opened my eyes and there right in front of my nose was a bee looking at me with great interest. Then, as if deciding that I would not be a suitable source of nectar, or whatever it is that bees seek, it buzzed the louder and veered off to some flower sheltering in the shade of a tree. I could hear it droning away there as it busily probed into the flower, and then it came out backwards and I saw that its legs and body were covered in yellow pollen.

It was pleasant here, reclining beneath the trees by the side of the river Thames at Thames Ditton, facing the great Palace of Hampton Court. My attention wandered and I suppose I dozed. Whatever it was I suddenly became aware of a noise in the distance. I had visions of the Royal

Barge coming down from the Tower of London and carrying Queen Elizabeth the First with her then-favourite boyfriend and the retinue of servants which seemed inevitable in royal circles.

There was music aboard the Royal Barge, and it seemed incongruous to me to have such music when coming up the Thames, but I could hear the splashing of oars, and the creaking of rollocks. There was much giggling and I thought to myself in my half-sleep state that surely people in early Elizabethan days did not behave as modern teenagers so.

I opened my eyes and there just coming around the bend was a large punt filled with teenagers and with a gramophone aboard as well as a radio, both were blaring out different tunes. They rowed along chattering away, everyone seemed to be talking on a different subject, no one was taking any notice of anyone else. They went along past Hampton Court and disappeared from my sight, and for a time again all was peace.

I thought again of the great Queen Elizabeth and of her journeys from the Tower of London to Hampton Court; nearly opposite to where I lay on the bank was the site where they used to have a landing jetty. The rowers used to come close and then ropes would be thrown and the Barge pulled in gently so as not to upset the Queen's balance because she was not a very good sailor, not even on the Thames! Hampton Court itself was a place that I found fascinating. I visited it often, and even under some unusual conditions, and I could see clearly that the place was indeed haunted with the spirits of those whose bodies had so long ago departed.

But there was much talking going on behind me, and I turned round and saw four people there. "Oh my goodness," said a woman, "you were so still—you haven't moved for the last ten minutes—that we thought you were dead!" With that they moved on, talking and talking and talking. The world, I thought, had too much noise, everyone had too much talk and too little to say. With that thought in mind I glanced about me. There were a few boats on the river Thames in front of me. Just down to the left of me was an old man who looked as if he might have been Father Time himself. He was stuck there like an old tree trunk. He had a pipe in his mouth and a faint haze of smoke was coming from it. Tied to a stick in front of him he had a fishing rod, the float of which—red and white— bobbed about just in front of me. I watched him for a short time, he didn't move either, and I wondered what people really saw in fishing. I came to the conclusion that it was just an excuse on the part of some elderly people so that they could keep still and meditate, think of the past, and wonder what the future held for them.

The future? I looked at my watch in alarm, and then hurried to get to my feet and mount the old bicycle which had been lying beside me on the bank.

With more haste than usual I pedalled off down the road and around to the right, and so on the way to West Molesey where the Unemployment Exchange was.

But no, there was no employment for me, no offer of a job. It seemed there were too many people and too few jobs, and as one man told me so bluntly, "Well mate, you left your job and you didn't have to, so as you left it and you didn't have to, you don't get paid nothing, see. So it stands to reason that the government ain't going to pay a fellow what left 'is job because he had a job before he left it, so you won't get no dole, and so long as you don't get no dole this here Exchange won't get you no job. The Exchange keeps its jobs for those who've got dole because if they get the fellow a job they don't have to pay him dole and so their statistics look better."

I tried commercial employment agencies, those places where you go and pay money, and where in theory they find you a job. My own experience may have been particularly unfortunate, but in spite of trying quite a number none of them ever offered me a job.

I managed to get just odd things to do around Thames Ditton and the district. I was able to do certain medical work which the orthodox physician could not do or would not do, and I thought—well, I am a fully qualified medical man and I've got the papers to prove it so why don't I try to get registered in England?

Sometime later I approached the General Medical Council unofficially. Actually I went to their place and told them all about it. They told me that—yes, I had all the qualifications but unfortunately Chungking was now in the hands of the Communists and, they said, I just could not expect my qualifications to be recognised as they were obtained in a Communist country.

I produced my papers, and shoved it straight under the Secretary's nose. I said, "Look, when these papers were prepared China was not a Communist country, it was an ally of England, France, the U.S.A., and many other countries. I fought for peace just the same as people in England fought for peace, and just because I was in a different country does not mean to say that I haven't got feelings the same as you have." He hummed and hawed and grunted around, and then he said, "Come back in a month's time. We'll see what can be arranged. Yes, yes, I quite agree, your qualifications are such that they should be recognised. The only thing impeding such recognition is that Chungking is now a city in a Communist country."

So I left his office and went to the Hunterian Museum to look at all the specimens in bottles, and I thought then how amazing it was that humans everywhere were—humans everywhere, they all functioned in roughly the same way and yet if a person was trained in one country he was not considered qualified to treat people in a different country. It was all beyond me.

But jobs were difficult indeed to obtain, and the cost of living at Thames Ditton was quite excessive. I found that as a married man, which in theory I was, expenses were far, far more than when I had to manage alone.

At this stage of the book perhaps I might take a moment to answer some of those people who write to me horribly offensively asking why should I, a lama of Tibet, live with a woman—have a wife. Well, all you "ladies" who write so offensively let me tell you this; I am still a monk, I still live as a monk, and possibly some of you

172

"ladies" have indeed heard of celibate bachelors who have a landlady or a sister with whom they live without necessarily thinking of THAT! So "ladies," the answer is—no, I don't!

But the time had come to leave Thames Ditton, and we moved nearer into London because by my own efforts I had made a job available for myself. I came to the conclusion that as the body that I now occupied was living "overtime" there were no opportunities for it. The former occupant of the body, I saw by the Akashic Record, really and truly had been going to commit suicide, and that would have completed all the opportunities which his vehicle, his body, would have had. Thus, no matter how hard I tried I could never take a job which another person could do; the only employment that I could take would be that which I generated for myself. Now, I don't propose to say what employment that was, nor where I did it because it is nothing to do with this story, but it proved to be adequate to supply our immediate wants and to keep us going. But I must tell you one thing which irritated me immensely, again it was connected with my old enemies the police. I was driving through South Kensington with an anatomical figure in the back of a car. It was one of those figures which appear in dress shops or which are sometimes provided for the training of surgical fitters. This figure was in the back of the car, and when I had started out it had been covered up with cloth but I drove with the window open and I suppose the draught had blown part of the cloth off the figure.

I was driving along quite peacefully thinking of what I was going to do next when suddenly there was a loud blare beside me, which nearly made me jump through the roof. I looked in the mirror and I found two figures gesticulating at me, pointing me to pull in to the side of the road. There were a lot of cars parked at the side of the road so I drove in a little to try to find a place where I could stop. The next thing was, this police car—for such it was—tried to ram me thinking, they said, that I was attempting to escape—at fifteen miles an hour in traffic!

173

Well, I stopped just where I was, holding up the traffic, and I couldn't care less about how cross the people in the other cars were, so I just stopped there. The police motioned for me to get out and come to them, but I thought —no, they want to see me, I don't want to see them, so I just sat. Eventually one policeman got out with his truncheon all ready in his hand. He looked as if he was going to face a firing squad or something, he really did look frightened. Slowly he came up to my side of the car walking more or less sideways presumably to make less of a target in case I started shooting. Then he looked into the back of the car and turned a bright red.

"Well, officer, what is it? What am I supposed to have done?" I asked him. The policeman looked at me and he really did look silly, he looked absolutely sheepish. "I'm sorry, sir," he said, "but we were told that a man was driving around and a naked woman's legs were showing through the back window."

I reached in to the back and pulled the cloth right off the figure, and then I said, "Well, officer, show me any sign of life in this model. Show me how she has been killed. Take a good look at her." And then I covered the figure more carefully. The policeman went back to his car and all the cars behind us were hooting away as if they were trying to fill a concert hall or something. Feeling thoroughly bad tempered I drove off.

There was another occasion with the police which may raise a smile; I had an office in London and it was very near an underground tube station. My wife often used to come and visit me round about lunch time, and when she was leaving I used to look out of the window just to see that she safely crossed that busy London street.

One day I was just getting ready to finish up and go home when there was a loud official knock at the door. I got up and went to the door and there there were two very large policemen. One said, "We want to know what you are doing here." I turned and let them come into my office. He looked about with interest and his associate got ready to act as witness. Everywhere the chief policeman looked his associate looked also.

I invited them to be seated, but no, they would not be seated, they were there on official business they told me. They said they thought I was engaged in some illicit activity and that I was giving signals to some gang.

This really shocked me, in fact I was almost stunned with amazement, and I just could not understand what they were talking about. "Whatever do you mean?" I exclaimed. The chief policeman said, "Well, it has been reported to us that you make strange signals at about midday and we have kept watch and we have seen those strange signals. To whom are you signalling?"

Then it dawned on me and I started to laugh. I said, "Oh good God, whatever is the world coming to? I am merely waving to my wife when I watch to see that she crosses the road safely and enters the tube station."

He said in reply, "That cannot be so, you cannot see the station from here." Without another word I got up from my chair, opened the window which was just to my right, and said, "Look and see for yoursefl." They looked at each other and then together they went to the window and looked out. Sure enough, just as I said, there was the underground station opposite. They both changed colour a bit, and I said—to make them change colour a bit more— "Oh yes, I've seen you two fellows, you were in that block of flats opposite, I saw you trying to hide behind the curtains. I wondered what you were up to."

The chief policeman then said, "You occupy the floor beneath this office. We have information that you are engaged in sexual activities in that flat below." I had had enough of this, and I said, "All right, come downstairs with me and see all the naked females for yourself." They were not at all happy with my attitude and they wondered what they had done wrong.

Together we went down a flight of stairs and I unlocked a big showroom, the windows of which were heavily curtained with expensive lace net.

Above the curtained windows there were small ventilators about a foot square which, of course, were not curtained.

I went to one lay figure and picked it up, and said, "Look, if a person is carrying this around, putting it from here to here"—I demonstrated—"a prying nosey-parker of an old woman who lives in that flat opposite might think it is a nude body."

I rapped on the figures and said, "All right, take a look at them, do they look obscene to you?"

The policemen changed their tune completely, and the senior one said, "Well, I am sorry you have been troubled, sir, I really am most sorry, but we received a complaint from the sister of a very senior police officer saying that strange things are happening here. We are quite satisfied with what we have seen. You will not be troubled again."

Well, I was! I had to go to my office one evening at about seven o'clock and I unlocked the doors and went in, as I had a perfect right to do. I did the bit of work that I had to do, and then left. As I locked the door behind me two policemen seized me quite roughly and tried to hustle me to a police car. But I knew my rights and I asked for an immediate explanation. They told me that it had been reported (yes, it was the same woman!) that a sinister-looking man (that's me!) had been seen to break into the building, so they were waiting for me. They would not believe that I had a right to be there, so I unlocked the office again and we went in, and I had actually to call the estate agent who had rented me the place, and he identified me by my voice. Once again the police looked silly and departed without a word.

Soon after that I decided that there was no point in staying in such an office where it was obvious that the old biddy opposite had nothing better to do with her time than imagine that she was a policewoman reporting all manner of imaginary criminal offences. So I left that office and went elsewhere.

Again, I did certain psychological work among people who could get no assistance from orthodox medicine and I did quite well, I really did. I cured a number of people but then one day there was a man who tried to blackmail me. So I learned that unless one was actually registered one was too much at the mercy of people who would gladly get all the assistance they could and then try to blackmail one. But the blackmailer—well, he didn't get his way after all!

Just at this time a young lady came into our life, came into our life of her own accord, of her own free will. We regarded her as a daughter and still do, and she is still with us. But her destiny, she felt, was such that she had to live with us, and that she did. Later the press were to make much of this, trying to say that it was a case of the eternal triangle; nothing could have been firmer than the truth. We were standing "on the square" instead of "in the eternal triangle."

At about this time I was introduced to an authors' agent. I thought I was going to get a job with him reading and commenting upon authors' typescripts, but no, he knew a bit of my story and very very much against my own will I allowed myself to be persuaded into writing a book. One cannot be too particular when starvation is just around the corner, you know, and starvation wasn't just around the corner, it was knocking hard on the door.

So I wrote a book, and then certain authors who were jealous at my knowledge of Tibet tried to trace me up. They got all manner of detective agencies, and one agency indeed put an advertisement in either The Times or The Telegraph of London advertising for Lobsang Rampa; he should write to such-and-such an address where something very good was waiting for him.

I knew this was a catch, and so I told my agent, Mr. Cyrus Brooks. He got his son-in-law to phone to see what it was all about. Yes, it was indeed a catch. An author in Germany was mightily peeved that I had written about Tibet when he thought that was his own private inviolable province, and so he tried to have me traced up so that he could decide what action he could take against me.

At about this time people connected with the young lady who was living with us took a dislike thinking that I had led her astray—I hadn't—and they also had a private detective trying to find out about me. But this poor fellow —well, it seems to me that he wasn't very bright, he never even tried to get in contact with me. I wonder if he was afraid or something. But instead of asking me outright as a man he relied on hearsay evidence, and as anyone should know, hearsay evidence is not legal evidence is it? But the two sides came together and they went to some press reporter who wasn't very popular with his fellows. They tried a few traps which I saw through, but when later we had moved to Ireland these people made a great campaign against me in the press, saying that I was doing black magic rites in the bottom of the house, that I had a secret temple, that I was guilty of all manner of sex orgies, etcetera, and that at some time in my career I had been in trouble with the police. Well, that was easy, I had always been in trouble with the police, but I had never been charged with anything, and I had never truly done anything worth police attention. But there is no point in stirring up old troubles and raking up ashes which should be burned out, but I want here to pay testimony to the husband of the young lady. He was and is a gentleman, he is a very good man, he is still our friend, and as he well knew and, indeed, as he testified, the statements about me were quite quite wrong.

No, I am saying no more about this, nothing about the press, nothing about the relatives of the young lady. She is still with us, still with us as a loved daughter. So there you are, that's all there is to that.

When all this happened we had moved to Ireland, and one thing and another had conspired to ruin my health. I had coronary thrombosis, and it was thought that I was going to die, but the press made life so hideous that we had to leave Ireland, which we did with extreme reluctance. I had many friends there, and I still have those selfsame friends.

We left Ireland and went to Canada where we are now. We moved about Canada quite a lot, we went to different cities, went to different provinces. But at last we had a letter in the mail which offered a lot.

In the mail one day there came quite a thick letter. The stamps were from a country of which I knew—at that time—remarkably little. It was from Uruguay, the country in South America which rests between Argentina and Brazil.

The letter was interesting. It told me that the writer was the head of a big company where they did printing, book publishing—everything. I was asked to go to Montevideo at the expense of that company, and I could continue my work there, I would be provided with secretaries, typists, translation services—in fact everything that I wanted. The writer sent me a photograph of himself looking quite impressive behind a big desk with an I.B.M. typewriter in front of him, a lot of books behind him, and, I think, a Phillips dictating machine there as well.

We discussed it, "we" being my wife and our adopted daughter, and after quite a time we thought that it would be a good idea. So we made all the necessary inquiries and at long last, because formalities took a time, we got on a train at Fort Erie, Ontario, Canada, for the trip to New York. We were told that we were going to be passengers aboard a Moore McCormack freighter, one which normally took twelve passengers.

In New York everything, as usual, was bustle and commotion. We stayed the night at one of the big hotels and the next morning we set off for the Moore McCormack dock in New York Harbour, and I was highly amused when I found that that dock was one right opposite the one to which I had made my swim so many years ago, it seemed. However, I said nothing, because there is not much point in raking up bitter memories, but, I confess, I kept quite a look out for river police.

We went aboard the ship and found our staterooms, and so late that night with four locomotives loaded aboard on the deck we steamed away to first Vittoria in Brazil. There we went up a long inlet before we arrived at a very picturesque, very hot little community. That was our first port of call. Then we went down to a place nearby so that

179

the locomotives—they were diesel locomotives for the Brazilian railroads—could be unloaded.

There were two or three more stops in Brazil until we were cleared for Montevideo in Uruguay. But as we approached Montevideo, actually we were at Punta del Este, the Captain was informed by radio that we could not land in Montevideo because there was a dock strike on, so we went to Buenos Aires first and we stayed in that port for about a week. It was quite a busy port, and we saw an enormous number of foreign ships come in. German ones seemed to be the most popular ones, and quite a lot of ships, it seemed, were going straight up the river which forms the frontier between Argentina and Uruguay. We were told that a few miles further up there was a great meat packing plant, the plant of Fray Bentos.

At last, though, we were cleared to leave port and down we went along the Rio de Plata, and at long last we came to Montevideo, our destination. We got into the outer harbour and the ship had to drop anchor. There had been a strike and a whole fleet of ships was assembled, and they had to be attended to first because they were there first, so we stayed aboard ship for about a week. At last the ship was allowed to enter harbour and we went ashore.

Our hopes were completely dashed, however, because we found that the man with an immense business did not have such an immense business after all. Instead—well, to put it at its kindest, he was a man with ideas which did not always work out.

It was very expensive living in Montevideo. They seemed to have a peculiar idea there that everything had to be paid for in American dollars so, in effect, taking into consideration the rate of exchange, we were paying fantastic sums for even basic items. However we stayed there for a year and a half, then we found there were all manner of strikes and increasing restrictions on foreigners, so we decided to leave.

It is most unfortunate that we had to leave because Montevideo was a nice place indeed. The people for the most part—except for the strikers!—were very pleasant,

180

very courteous, and it was like being in a European city. It was a beautiful city with a wonderful harbour and beaches. For a very short time we stayed at a place called Carrasco, quite near the airport. This had one terrible defect in that very fine sand from the immense beaches was always getting blown into the houses, so as we were also too far from the city centre we moved to an apartment building which overlooked the lighthouse.

A few miles out in the approaches to the harbour there was a wrecked ship. It had been a quite large passenger liner and for some reason the ship had been sunk just off the main entrance, and there it remained. At low tide one could just see the main deck, at high tide the bridge and the bridge deck was still above water. We saw quite a lot of smuggling going on here because the ship was used as a "drop" for smugglers.

There were many beautiful sights in Montevideo including a high eminence just across the other side of the harbour. This was known as "the Mountain" and there was a sort of fort, which was a local tourist attraction, right at its peak.

The British had done much to modernise Montevideo. They had started its bus service, and they had also started the gas works, and one of the advantages of that was that so many people had a smattering of English.

One day when we had moved to yet another apartment closer into the city centre the sky turned black and for a time everything turned bitterly cold. Then there came a cyclone. Three of us struggled to close our open window and as we were there congregated, pushing our shoulders hard against the window, we saw an amazing sight indeed; the bus station roof just below us suddenly vanished, all the sheets of corrugated iron were flying through the air as if they were made of tissue paper. We looked down and saw all the buses there and workers were gazing up wide-mouthed and with wide eyes.

A really amusing sight—for us—was when hens, which had been kept on the flat roofs of houses in Montevideo, were blown straight up in the air and crossed street after

181

street in probably the only flight they ever had in their lives. It really is an astonishing sight to see hens go flying by with their wings tight to their sides!

A sight which really made me amused was when a whole clothes line laden with newly-washed clothes went sailing by. The line was as tight and as stiff as an iron bar, and sheets and "unmentionables" were hanging straight down as if in still air. I have seen many cyclones, whirlwinds, etcetera, but this from my point of view was quite the most amusing.

But Montevideo was losing its charm, so we decided to return to Canada because of the various groups of Communists who were making trouble. In many ways I am sorry for it because I think I would rather live in Uruguay than in most other places. They have a different mentality there. They call themselves the Oriental Republic of Uruguay. It is a poor country with wonderful ideals, but ideals so idealistic that they were impractical.

We returned to Canada by sea, and then there was the question of making money so I had to write another book. My health was deteriorating a lot, and that was the only thing I could do.

During my absence I found that a person had written a book on material I had written for an English magazine some years previously. He was a very peculiar sort of person, whenever he was tackled or threatened with a law case he conveniently went bankrupt and friends or relatives "bought" his business, so there was not much redress, in fact there was none.

One of the big troubles I have had since "The Third Eye" is the number of people who write "Approved by Lobsang Rampa," and just put labels to that effect on the goods they supply. All that is quite untrue; I do not "approve" things. Many people, too, have impersonated me, in fact, on quite a number of occasions I have had to call in the police. There was, for example, a man in Miami who wrote to a bookseller in San Francisco in my name, he actually signed my name. He wrote a lot of "Holy Joe" stuff, which I never do, and he ordered a lot of books to be sent to him. Quite by chance I wrote to the bookseller at the same time from Vancouver and he was so amazed at getting a letter apparently from me and in British Columbia that he wrote to me and asked how I was moving so quickly. So it came out that this fellow had been for some time ordering goods in my name and not paying. As I said, if anyone is fool enough to take as "me" the gobblegook that this fellow had been writing deserves to get caught. There have been others such as the man who retired to a mountain cave, sat cross-legged with darn little clothing on him, and pretended to be me. He advised teenagers to have sex and drugs, saying that it was good for them. But the press, of course, seized on such incidents and made quite a commotion, and even when it was proved that these impostors were impersonating me the press never got round to reporting the actuality of what happened. I am utterly, utterly, utterly opposed to suicide. I am utterly, utterly opposed to drugs, and I am utterly, utterly opposed to the press. I think that the average pressman is not fitted to report things on metaphysics or the occult, they do not have the knowledge, they do not have the spirituality, and, in my opinion, they just do not have the brain power.

After a time in Fort Erie, to which we returned from South America, we went to Prescott, Ontario, where we lived in a small hotel. The Manager of that hotel was an extremely fine man indeed. We stayed there a year, and during the whole of that year there was never at any time the slightest disagreement or slightest lack of harmony between "management" and us. His name was Ivan Miller, and he was a real gentleman and I wish I knew his address now to again express my appreciation of all the efforts he made. He was a great big man, huge in fact, and he had been a wrestler, yet he could be more gentle than most women.

CHAPTER ELEVEN

It was good to be back in Canada to get what was then a reliable mail service. There had been quite a lot of trouble in Uruguay and one particular incident which really made me foam with fury was when, as an author, I had a lot of mail sent to me and the post office in Montevideo would not let me have it. I had my adopted name, and I also had the name under which I wrote, T. Lobsang Rampa, and the post office officials in Montevideo were quite adamant in not letting me have mail for two names. Their idea was that a person must be a crook if they had to have two names, and so I gave the matter much thought and came to the conclusion that I was far better known as T. Lobsang Rampa. Then I went to the post office and said I wanted the mail for T. Lobsang Rampa and they could return the rest.

Then they had to see my papers. My papers had the wrong name on them, so I was unable to get my mail. Eventually I had to go to a lawyer—an 'abogado'—and have a Change of Name Deed drawn up. It had to be done legally, and there were many many stamps on the document, after which notice had to be given in an Uruguayan legal newspaper all about the name change. When all those formalities were completed then I could get mail in the name of T. Lobsang Rampa but I was forbidden to use the other name.

Now, of course, my name has been legally changed in Canada as well to T. Lobsang Rampa, and while we are on the subject of officialdom, bureaucracy, etcetera—I am now a Canadian subject. I took out Canadian naturalisation and, here again, the formalities were truly amazing. But there seem to be formalities in everything nowadays, I have been trying to get the Old Age Pension, to which I am entitled, but bureaucracy is such that apparently I cannot get it—or so the officials tell me—unless I give the exact address and the exact dates of arriving and leaving every place I have been in Canada. Well, I have been to an amazing number of places from Windsor to Prescott, to Montreal, Saint John, New Brunswick, Halifax, all the way on to Vancouver back to Calgary, etcetera, and I should have thought that I was well enough known as a Canadian citizen and with a passport, etcetera, but apparently that does not suit the bureaucracy-mad officials. So the matter is "still pending." I sounds more like a rotten apple than anything else, doesn't it?

Last night I was very unwell indeed and late in the night I awakened from an uneasy doze and found clustered around me a group of those who were my associates, lamas from Tibet. They were in the astral, and they were agitating for me to get out of the body and go over and discuss things with them. "What is the matter with you all?" I asked. "If I feel any worse than I do now I shall be over there permanently." The Lama Mingyar Dondup smiled and said, "Yes, that's what we are afraid of. We want you to do something else first."

When one has done astral travel for as many years as I have there is nothing to it, it is easier than stepping out of bed, so I just slipped out of this body and went into the astral. Together we walked to the side of a lake on which there were many water birds playing. Here in the astral, you know, creatures have no fear whatever of Man, so these birds were simply playing in the water. We sat on a moss-covered bank, and my Guide said, "You know, Lobsang, there isn't enough detail given about transmigration. We wanted you to say something about peoples who have used transmigration." Well, the day in the astral was too pleasant to be much of a cross-patch, so I indicated that on the morrow I would get to work again before the book was finished.

It was very pleasant, though, being in the astral, away from pain, away from worries and all the rest of it. But, as I was reminded, people do not go to Earth for pleasure,

185

they go because they have something to learn or something to teach.

Today, then, is another day, the day when I have to write something even more about transmigration.

In the days of Atlantis and—oh yes!—there really was Atlantis, it is not just a figment of a writer's imagination; Atlantis was real. But, in the days of Atlantis there was a very high civilization indeed. People "walked with Gods." The Gardeners of the Earth were ever watching developments on Atlantis. But those who are watched are wary of the watchers, and so it came about that the Gardeners of the Earth used the process of transmigration so that they could keep a more subtle form of watch.

A number of bodies of suitable vibrations were used by the spirits of Gardeners, and then they could mingle with humans and find out just what the humans really thought of the Gardeners and were they plotting.

The Gardeners of the Earth who looked after that mysterious civilisation known as the Sumerians also had tutors come to the Earth by transmigration. It was altogether too slow to have great space ships cross the void taking such a long time. By transmigration it could be done in a matter of seconds.

The Egyptians, also, were largely controlled and entirely taught by higher Entities who entered into specially cultivated bodies, and when those bodies were not actually being used by the Entities they were carefully cleaned, wrapped up, and put aside in stone boxes. The ignorant Egyptian natives catching brief glances of the ceremonies came to the conclusion that the Gardeners were preserving the bodies, and so those who had witnessed such proceedings rushed home to their priests and told all that they had seen.

The priests then thought that they would try such things, and when a high enough person died they wrapped him up in bandages, coated him with spices, and all the rest of it, but they found that the bodies decayed. Then they came to the conclusion that it was the intestines, the heart, liver and lungs which caused the decaying, so all those parts

186

were removed and put in separate jars. It is a good thing they were not preparing the hosts for incoming spirits because the hosts would indeed have been a gutless lot, wouldn't they?!

Of course, some of the embalming—so called—was when a sick space man or space woman was being put into the state of suspended animation so that he or she could be removed to a space ship and taken elsewhere for treatment.

There have been quite a number of well-known leaders on this Earth who were Entities transmigrated into Earth-bodies, Abraham, Moses, Gautama, Christ, and then that well-known genius of geniuses, Leonardo da Vinci. The inventions of Leonardo da Vinci are legend, and he enhanced the knowledge of this world very very greatly. He, as I suppose anyone would agree, possessed skills and sciences far beyond the knowledge of Earth people. The person known as Leonardo da Vinci had been an illegitimate child without any special advantages. Who knows? He might even have been the son of a plumber! The body of the person who became Leonardo da Vinci was of such a degree of vibration that a very high Entity could take it over and do all those things which no human could have done.

In all seriousness, I say that if the people of this world would only listen to those who can actually do transmigration there would be a wonderful chance of space exploration. Think of all the worlds there are. Think of being able to visit a world in a matter of seconds. Some of the worlds can never be visited by orthodox humans because the atmosphere may be wrong, the climate may be wrong, or the gravity may be wrong. But when a person is doing transmigration he can take over the body of any native of the planet, and so then can explore the planet without any difficulties whatever.

Humans, well versed in the science of transmigration could enter the bodies of animals so that they could be studied effectively. This has been done before, it has been done frequently before, and because of a racial memory

187

there are certain false beliefs that humans are reborn as animals. They are not—ever. Nor are animals born as humans. Animals are not inferior to humans, either. But because there is a racial memory of Gardeners of the Earth taking over the bodies of certain animals, the knowledge of that has lingered on in a distorted form. Thus it is that good religions are debased.

We have travelled extensively in Canada. I have been from Windsor, Ontario, to Fort Erie and on to Prescott, and then we went to Saint John, N.B. For a time, as you can read in others of my books, we lived quite happily in New Brunswick, in the very pleasant city beside the sea. But as my accountant said, an author must travel, so we moved to Montreal and we lived in Habitat for some time. Habitat is that funny looking collection of houses piled one on top of the other like children's building bricks. Anyway, it was quite a nice place to live, and in fact we liked it so much that after we had left it we later returned to it. Here again, in Montreal there were always strikes, there was a language difficulty, too, because the French-Canadians were not at all friendly to those who did not speak French, and my own firm opinion has always been that Canada was an English speaking country and I refused to speak French.

Soon came the time when we moved again, this time to Vancouver, British Columbia, where we lived in a hotel, actually a hotel which also had apartments to it. Vancouver has gone down a lot lately under what I consider to be a most horrible form of government. And another complaint against Vancouver is that "no pets" was the sign everywhere, and as one hotel keeper once said, pets had never hurt his business but children had and so had drunks and so had people who smoked in bed and set the place on fire.

I have moved about a lot in my life. I have learned much, and there are certain things I "wish" could be—

I wish, for instance, that there could be a censorship of the press because I have seen so much misery caused by inaccurate press reports. I am glad to note that now many

many more people are obviously agreeing with me on this, because the accuracy of the press is often in doubt nowadays.

The predictions made about me so very very long ago have been utterly accurate. It was predicted that even my own people would turn against me. Well, they have—they have indeed, because in my time of trouble no one came forward to help me or to attest the truth of my story, and true that story is.

I had so many hopes about helping Tibet. I thought, for example, that with recognition I would be able to speak for Tibet before the United Nations. I hoped that with recognition I could have had a radio programme about free Tibet, but no, no help whatever has been given to me by the people of Tibet who have left that country. Sadly enough it is their loss as well as mine. So much good could have been done. My name is widely known, it has been conceded that I can write, it has been stated also that I can talk. I wanted to use both in the service of Tibet, yet they have not been at all anxious to recognise me, just the same as in the past a Dalai Lama would not recognise the Panchen Lama and vice versa. It is just the same, we will say, as one political leader ignoring the existence of another. But I get a vast number of letters, on this day, for example, I had one hundred and three. It has often been much more, and the letters come from all over the world. I learn things which are closed to many, and I have been told, rightly or wrongly, that the present people who escaped from Tibet cannot "recognise" me because another religious faction who is helping them would be cross. I have all the evidence that that is so, actually. But—well—there is no point in starting a miniature religious war, is there?

It is mainly the lower orders of refugees who seem to be opposed to me. I had a letter some months ago from an important man who had been to see the Dalai Lama and had discussed me. The Dalai Lama, it was reported to me, had extended an invitation to me to return to the Potala when it was freed from Communist aggression.

189

And just a few weeks back our adopted daughter (we "name no names," remember?) received a letter saying that the Dalai Lama was very concerned about Dr. Rampa's health, and the Dalai Lama was praying for him daily. That letter is now in the possession of my publishers.

Another "wish" I have is this; there are quite a number of occult bodies about, some of them claiming to be very very ancient even though they were started again by an advertising man just a few years ago. But my complaint is this; if all these people are so holy—so good—so devoted to spiritual enlightenment then why cannot we all get together because if they are truly genuine they would realise that all paths lead Home.

A number of students from some of these cult-colleges have asked me why I did not get in touch with Group so-and-so or Group something else, and the answer is that I have done, and I have had some shockingly insulting replies from these groups all because they are jealous or because they have been poisoned by the press. Well, I do not see it that way at all. I maintain that it does not matter what religion one belongs to, it does not matter how one studies the occult. If people are genuine they would be able to work together.

Some years ago I was approached by a man who was the founder of a so-called Tibetan Science. He wrote to me and suggested that we could make a lot of money if I joined with him and he used my name. Well, I do not do things like that, I do not go in for this work as a money-making gimmick. My beliefs are my everyday beliefs and I live according to the code under which I was taught.

I would like to see many of these so-called metaphysical societies or Orders licensed after careful examination. So many of them are fakes just out to gather money. I know of one particular group who admit quite freely that they take what they consider to be the best from a whole load of writers and hash it up as something quite different. Well, that is dishonest.

This is a good opportunity to tell you once again—in case you start at the back end of this book instead of the front, as so many do—that all my books are absolutely true. Everything that I have written is fact. Every metaphysical experience I write about I can do, and it is my most sincere wish that there will come a time when people will indeed recognise the truth of my books because I still have a lot to teach people. Nowadays, because of the lies propagated by the press, I have been treated as a leper or pariah. Many people "dip into" my books and then write things as if it was their own idea. Some time ago I listened with great satisfaction on short waves to a long extract from one of my books, and then at the end of the reading I was almost stunned to hear that authorship has been ascribed to some woman who can hardly sign her name!

Believe me, then, all my books are true, and I believe I have the system whereby peoples of this world can visit other worlds in safety.

I want to thank Mrs. Sheelagh M. Rouse who has typed fifteen of these books. I typed the first one. She has typed them without a groan, too.

Another thing in which you may be interested is this; Mrs. Rampa has now nearly completed a book giving her side of all this affair. If you want to know about it—well, you will have to watch for advertisements, won't you? Or you can write to:-

Mr. E. Z. Sowter,
A. Touchstone Ltd.,
33 Ashby Road,
Loughborough, Leics.,
England.

So ends Book Four
As It Is Now!